THE LAW

OF

THE TERRITORIES.

PHILADELPHIA:
PRINTED BY C. SHERMAN & SON.
1859.

CONTENTS.

PREFACE.

THE first of the two essays in this volume was begun with the intention of making it an article for the North American and United States Gazette, of this city. The subject, however, expanded before the author as he advanced, and grew, as he followed its lead, to a size too large for a newspaper. The second essay, on "Popular Sovereignty in the Territories," was published in the above-named Journal, February 24th, 1858, with the signature of Cecil, and formed one of a series of essays on Southern politics, for which the courtesy of the Editor of that paper allowed the author the use of his columns. The two are now presented to the public in the present shape, in the hope that, if the principles they assert and attempt to explain are correct, they may be of some use in guiding opinion on a subject of great importance, the discussion of which is likely, at this moment, to excite general interest.

Some weeks after the last written of these essays was

finished, an event occurred which has given increased significance to the topics they treat. A band of some fifteen to twenty desperate men surprised the village of Harper's Ferry, seized on the United States Arsenal, made prisoners of a number of prominent gentlemen in the neighborhood, stopped the railway trains, and placed themselves, after committing these outrages, in an attitude of defiance to the law and its officers. This extraordinary feat was performed by fifteen white men and four negroes. As soon as news of it could be known, troops were promptly sent to the scene of action by the President of the United States, by the Governor of Virginia, and by the State of Maryland. After a short conflict, in which, however, several lives were sacrificed, the insurgents were captured and taken to a town in Virginia for trial. Upon this trial the eyes of the nation are now fixed. Its progress is reported in every newspaper throughout the land. The place where it is conducted is like a garrisoned town. The wounded prisoner, the leader of the band, is escorted to and from the court-house by a military guard. Alarm reigns throughout the State of Virginia and adjacent country, whose citizens are arming spontaneously, and whose magistrates are holding counsel over the public safety. That nineteen men, by conduct however violent, should be able to excite such wide consternation and induce preparations so large and instant, may seem very surprising. Our cities are, unhappily, often the scenes of conflicts as serious, which are dealt with by the local police, and speedily forgotten. The fights and riots of the rowdy clubs in Baltimore alone, appear more momentous things in comparison. The excitement, the means of defence employed, and the interest created at a distance, seem out of all proportion to the event, until its true character is understood; but all surprise vanishes the moment it is known that the purpose of this little band of misguided men was to produce an insurrection of the slaves. If the laborers in a powder factory were seen to fly the building on the entrance of a single man, or to rush on him with frantic haste to put him out, no one would wonder at their conduct if told that he had a cigar in his mouth. The affair at Harper's Ferry therefore reveals a danger inherent in Southern society. The danger must be real, or such terror and active vigilance could not have been excited in a community proverbially high-spirited and brave, by a cause otherwise so insignificant. The people of the South are like the crew of a ship of war. They carry with them a magazine of explosive matter, which must be carefully guarded from even a casual spark.

But this event, in its causes and surrounding circumstances, has other meanings of grave national interest. Deplorable in itself, it is by no means an isolated fact, growing out of nothing and related to nothing. To regard it as the mere desperate freak of a madman, the powerless conception of one crazed brain, would be greatly to mistake its character. It is connected with the past, its true nature is displayed in the facts by which it was accompanied, and in the scenes of the passing hour, and it is connected, also, with the future, for good or for evil, as it shall be managed, and as the lessons it teaches shall be understood.

One important fact in the case is, that the motives and purposes, the ideas and passions, which prompted the extravagant enterprise of Brown, find sympathy and approval in a portion of Northern opinion. Whether he was aided and abetted by Northern men of influence in this particular deed, as asserted, remains to be seen; nor is it of much consequence in a general point of view. The startling and dangerous fact that, in some of the Northern States, numbers sufficiently large to have political and social power, to form constituencies, to exercise the sway of educated opinion, do, with more or less earnestness and enthusiasm, approve, if not of his act, of the feelings and principles that led him to act; do regard him as a martyr in a just cause, and would have rejoiced had he been successful, this fact is beyond dispute, and, however painful or alarming, it is well to look it in the face. Influential men, members of Congress, candidates for office, conductors of widely-circulating journals; men representing and guiding, and able to inflame a portion of public opinion, are among this number; and they are at this moment engaged, by nightly lectures and harangues in Northern cities, and by newspaper discussions, in appealing to the reason, the sympathies and passions of the people. It must be confessed that all this fire of feeling and of rhetoric is no safe neighbor for the powder magazine. No one can tell when or where or how a spark may be blown into it, or the frenzy of fanaticism may be incited to hurl a torch at it, as Brown did; or, indeed, whether even the distant din and concussion of all this turmoil, may not, by mysterious, electric sympathy, cause the spontaneous combustion of the sensitive, fulminating stuff which forms the foundation of Southern society. It is clear that it is of vital importance for the Southern people to have good neighbors; friends, not enemies; nay, if possible, allies and brethren—shipmates, interested, like themselves, in keeping the powder secure. A small number of Northern enemies is no safe thing for them. We have just seen that fifteen desperate men, their heads full of the most absurd theories, their hearts full of the wildest passions, were sufficient to strike no vain or weak terror into the State of Virginia, and make her gird on her sword in hot haste to meet a pressing danger. Who can say that had Brown been successful in rousing the Negroes, had made a stand but for a single day, thousands would not have crossed the border to join him, with what results of wide-spread mischief, is more easy than pleasant to imagine? And if a handful of poor, ignorant, and lawless men, are able to cause such perils, what effect would an army marching with legal banners, on a similar errand, produce? Disunion is a word of fear. Is it not strange that it should have been as yet pronounced only by the South?

The danger of insurrection and servile war belongs to the nature of slavery. In a country thinly settled, of large plantations and farms, and widely separated dwellings, where six millions of one race hold four millions of another race in subjection, and the two are interspersed and mingled together, there is risk at all times. It is, perhaps, not too much to assert, that the safety and tranquillity of Southern society depend on the fact that the Northern people are close at hand to aid in case of need, that the power of the General Government is ever ready for the same purpose. Four millions of barbarians, growing with tropical vigor, and soon to be eight millions, with tropical passions boiling in their blood, endowed with native courage, with sinews strung by toil and stimulated by the hope of liberty and unbounded license, are not to be trifled with. Take away from them the idea of an irresistible power in the North, ready at any moment to be invoked by their masters, or let them expect in the North, not enemies, but friends and supporters, which even now they are told every day by these masters they may expect, and how soon might a flame be lighted, which no power in the South could extinguish. If the South could be separated, geographically, from the North, standing armies and a complete military organization would at once become essential for its safety, and even these would be a doubtful protection from an insidious danger, lurking in every home, and ever ready to be roused by the very precautions taken against it. Slavery could not be maintained in Cuba but for the power of Spain. Had England withdrawn her protection from her West India Islands, the negroes would have emancipated themselves. When the government of France proclaimed opinions hostile to slavery, St. Domingo became Hayti. Withdraw from the South the invisible support which Northern strength gives to slavery, and Southern society would be in danger. Convert this Northern strength into an enemy, and at once, throughout the fertile and peaceful regions of the South, would arise a household horror, a fireside foe, a domestic terror more dreadful than war. War has its laws, its amenities, its mercies. It can be met in manful battle; it can be stopped by honorable submission; it spares the young and the aged, the sick and the feeble; it respects female honor; it commits no useless devastation; it does not overthrow law and government. But a servile insurrection, brute force unchained, brute passion stimulated by license and revenge, the tropical fury of the negro, of the mere animal man, let loose upon the wealth and refinement of a civilized and polished community, who shall describe the miseries, the manifold horrors of such a scourge? Almost as great an evil as a servile war, is the constant dread of it. When danger dwells under a man's roof, when his servants and laborers may be his enemies, whom it is unsafe even to seem to distrust, the sense of security which governments and laws are intended to produce, is destroyed. The enjoyment of life vanishes, all plans, purposes, and thoughts become absorbed in the one dominant idea of self-preservation, and society is ruled by a pervading terror. Such a society cannot prosper, cannot live. Industry, business, wealth, require the shelter of peace and order, and confidence in the stability of these. Capital, the most timid of all things, which scents peril from afar, and "shuts its coward gates on atomies," would quickly fly to safer regions for investment, and its owners would fly along with it. Love of country is strong, but love of life, love of family, are stronger. All men who had the means would, when the risk became serious, gather together what they were able of their estates and escape from a danger, which hovers over the hours of privacy and the scenes of domestic enjoyment, from an enemy with whom there can be no combat or treaty of peace, and which, if not entirely subdued and subjected, threatens evils worse than death. At length the white race, weakened, impoverished, dispirited, and demoralized, would fall an easy prey to the Negro, which has struck its roots so deeply into our soil, and grows on it with African vigor and luxuriance. It would be far better in all respects for the South to emancipate the slaves at once, and convert them into free laborers, working for hire, than to live in fear of them. Emancipation would be a very doubtful experiment for both races, however gradual and carefully guarded. Slavery with us is a mild institution and its yoke is easy. Under its generally kind and wholesome rule, the Negro flourishes, is industrious, temperate, orderly, and well cared for, at least in physical well-being. He could not take as good care of himself. With it, too, the South increases in wealth and power, and enjoys the blessings of peace and security. It would be rash and foolish and wicked, in the hope of realizing ideal visions, and to carry out to extreme conclusions the theories of abstract reasoning, to risk so much actual, practical good, so long as this state of things continues. But ideas have a subtle force, and find their way even into the mind of a Negro. No laws or guards can keep them out, or prevent their working after their kind, that is, producing action, after they get in. Should the idea that he is *wrongfully* a slave, and with it the spirit of insubordination, ever enter that dim region, the Negro intellect, and pervade it; should it ever happen that not love, not duty, not fidelity, but simply fear, shall hold him in subjection, then this man-merchandise of the Supreme Court will prove that it is human and linked by moral ties with humanity, by inspiring the distrust of which it is the object. No society can be founded on fear. Not iron fetters, but the golden chain of mutual confidence, of reciprocal benefit, is necessary to secure the obedience even of the Negro, and make him, four millions strong, a safe companion for the white race. The moment he becomes really dangerous, emancipation would be the only refuge for the South. Southern society could exist, could enjoy tranquillity, might even prosper after emancipation, just as the British West Indies have existed after it, and, according to late accounts, have prospered. If we may believe a recent article in the Edinburgh Review (April, 1859), the revenues of the islands have increased, the estates of the planters improved in productiveness and value, and the negroes, instead of becoming, as generally anticipated and reported, lazzaroni or banditti, fast relapsing into African barbarism, are now an industrious, orderly, contented, and thriving peasantry. If this be true, the fact is most important, and of deep interest to the moralist and social philosopher, though of no practical value in the politics of our country, as the subject is beyond the control of the Government. But there is no middle course. The negroes must be either free or absolutely and securely slaves. As the question of emancipation cannot be tried or even discussed by our Government; as an illegal attempt to make it would produce evils, compared with which all the evils of slavery, real or imputed, are blessings, it may be stated as a condition absolutely essential to the safety of the South and of all the vast interests that depend on it, that slavery be there so established and guarded, that it may inspire no dread; that the two races may live together in this relation without suspicion or fear; the one exercising just authority and kind protection, the other yielding cheerful obedience and faithful service, controlled moreover by a wholesome conviction that resistance or revolt is hopeless.

Under this state of things the South has prospered. Under no other is healthy life possible for it. It is impossible for the Southern people to hold four millions of Negroes as slaves, with the North as an enemy. Civil war would light the flames of servile war throughout the South. Even without disunion, it is impossible that the security and confidence essential to the industry, wealth, and happiness of civilized society, can exist in the South, if a considerable part of the Northern people are mischievously bent on exciting discontent, extravagant hopes, and the disposition to rebellion, among the Negroes. The spirit of insubordination is inconsistent with the feeling of security. Society cannot exist if palsied by a vague, indeterminate and constant dread of nameless horrors, haunting the fireside. It is a difficult thing to realize the truth that this danger does now exist in our country. It has been suddenly revealed by the tragedy at Harper's Ferry. Every newspaper teems with the proof of it. It is a fact, to be confronted and dealt with, that there is a body of men in the Northern States, formidable for its numbers, wealth, social influence, political power, talents, and zeal, willing to diffuse among the negroes ideas and aspirations inconsistent with their position as slaves; willing to afford them encouragement and sympathy, and the expectation of support, if not actual physical aid, in resistance and revolt. These men are able, if they cannot be checked, to destroy the South,—to destroy the Nation.

It is, therefore, clear that the security of slavery, and with it of Southern society, depends on the friendship of the North, which is its close neighbor, and must ever remain so, either as a friend or an enemy. In other words, *slavery depends on the opinion which the Northern people may have of it.* If they thought about it as the Southern people do, it would be in no danger whatever; and the nearer the sentiments of North and South on this subject can be brought together, the better for the interests of slavery. The extraordinary thing is, that notwithstanding this obvious truth, the conduct of Southern politicians seems to have been purposely intended for some years past to make the South and Slavery as odious as possible to the Northern people. The repeal of the Missouri Compromise let loose the spirit of discord, which that wise and just law had quelled. An exciting question which had been settled was opened, the demon of sectional passion was needlessly roused from its repose, and Kansas was offered to contending parties as an arena for their strife—Kansas, whence slavery is banished by the laws of Nature herself. The contest which then took place fixed upon that wild and remote region the eyes of the Nation. The whole people sympathized with one side or the other, and followed the progress of the struggle with eager interest.

The real conflict was soon transferred from Kansas to the elections throughout the country and to Washington. The events occurring in Kansas were quickly merged in the principles they involved; the quarrels and fights and respective merits of the rude settlers and the ruder Missourians, lost their importance when compared with the conduct of political parties and of public men. Then followed in rapid succession, the assault on Mr. Sumner, the invasion of Kansas by Missourians, the fraudulent election of a Territorial Legislature, the infamous laws of that Legislature, the decision in the case of Dred Scott, and, finally, the Lecompton Constitution, by which an attempt was made to force Slavery on the people of Kansas against their consent;—all of these either the acts of Southern politicians and their adherents, Northern Democrats, or approved, applauded, ratified, supported and used by them for party and sectional purposes. They were all violations of constitutional law, of settled usage, of moral obligations, and of principles dear to the American heart. They were all caused by Slavery. They were all intended to gain power for Slavery and the South. They were all prompted by Southern men for Southern interests and designs. They excited just and general indignation among the Northern people. Is it surprising that this feeling should, with many, be turned against Slavery itself, against the South, which the authors and supporters of these outrages professed to represent? Is it surprising, when the civil rights of Americans were violated for the sake of Slavery, that Slavery should become hateful to some of them? That, when the breaking of laws, when violence and bloodshed, were aided and abetted and cheered by Southern politicians for Southern purposes, resentment should be directed to the South? By these misdeeds the friends of the South were cooled and its enemies heated throughout the North. The mouths of its advocates were shut, and arguments not easily answered supplied to its foes. Enthusiasts against Slavery became fanatics; moderate men, enthusiasts, and the ranks of its ancient and faithful adherent,—the Democratic party,—were thinned by this fatal and reckless course of passion and folly and crime, which none could approve and few venture to defend. This is the real origin and cause of the deplorable event at Harper's Ferry. The desperate design of Brown was conceived amid the border warfare of Kansas. It was nourished and grew into a settled purpose and plan in the atmosphere of passion there excited, and was stimulated by the injuries he suffered. Revenge mingled with his fanaticism and pushed it on to action. But he was not alone in the feeling, though alone in the act. The sentiment which impelled him was shared by many in less degree, and now, when he has failed and is sentenced to death, his blind enthusiasm, his wild and extravagant opinions and hopes, still animate thousands, who regret his fate, sympathize in his principles, and would have exulted in his success. This dangerous flame of passion and doctrine has been kindled by the treatment of Kansas, and by the shameful decision in the case of Dred Scott, by which slaves, contrary to the general practice and sentiment of the South, are converted into mere property, and classed in the scale of God's creation, not as men, but things. The most repulsive aspect of Slavery is the one which Southern politicians have thus chosen to offer to the world and to the Northern people. The harangues of the Abolitionists ring with these topics. Chattel slavery, the outrages of the "border ruffians" in Kansas, and the Lecompton Constitution, form the texts of their inflammatory appeals at this moment, when the trial of Brown is going on in Virginia, whose people are mustering in arms as though they expected invasion every hour, and are thus teaching both to Negroes and Abolitionists the secret of their power. Distant Kansas has stretched out a long arm and struck the South a blow, feeble indeed, but sufficient to make it quiver and palpitate from end to end.

The South is a great power, rich in territory, in resources, in wealth, in numbers, in the spirit, energy, and intelligence of its people. Through these it has always influenced, and, for the most part, controlled the Government of this country. It is covered all over with the panoply of the Constitution, of laws, and of the vast interests of which it is the source and basis. The South rules the President, and Congress, and the Supreme Court. It has all kinds of influence, social, commercial, political. It dictates to Tammany Halls and to Empire Clubs, who echo its opinions with eager unanimity, and fulminate its decrees with active zeal. But, like Achilles, the South has a vulnerable point which its enemies have found out. They have aimed at this point a weak shaft by a feeble hand, and, suddenly, the whole ingenious armament of the Southern politicians, obedient Presidents, a submissive Congress, a pliant judiciary, responsive Tammany Halls, and active rowdy clubs, have become useless as the guns of a ship that has sprung aleak; they cannot keep out the sea, but may sink her into it, and the sooner they are thrown overboard the better.

The affair at Harper's Ferry has, however, shed a strong light upon a more cheering aspect of our affairs. If it has proved that there exists in the North opinions and passions which may become dangerous to the repose of Southern society, it has also shown that the great body of the Northern people are true and loyal to their country, and to the South as a part of it. There never was any reason to doubt this, though it has been constantly and obstinately denied by Southern politicians, who, to serve their own narrow designs, have industriously represented the North as united in hatred of Slavery, and bent on its destruction. But the truth is, the Abolitionists, though they have recently increased in numbers and influence, are comparatively insignificant. The real people, the conservative classes, who control and manage the great interests connected with Commerce, Manufactures, and Agriculture, appreciate too well the value of the Union, of Southern industry and production, to wish to see servile war, or the withering dread of it, desolate or weaken or impoverish the South, even if the higher motives of patriotism and humanity did not influence them. Their sentiments are proved by the unanimous burst of regret and indignation which the attempt made at Harper's Ferry has drawn from the whole country, with but few exceptions, without distinction of party. The lovers of order and peace, of industry and its rewards, of the security of property and all vested rights, are the true friends of the South. They are not the enemies of the cotton crop, or of the rice and sugar and tobacco which freight their ships, or employ their mills, and build up their cities; neither are they, or can they be, the enemies of that system of labor on which these interests are founded, provided they can honestly and conscientiously be its friends. They are bound to the South by a thousand sympathies and relations of interest and feeling, of commerce and marriage and friendship, and without these ties, stronger than the Constitution, the Union would be a rope of sand. These classes are the true allies of the planter. They are stronger than demagogues, or rowdy clubs, or the mobs of cities. But though they are the friends of the South, they will not be the tools of its politicians, nor can they behold, unmoved, the North insulted and oppressed, the Constitution of their country trampled in the dust, the principles of liberty and justice outraged, or the power of the Nation usurped and employed to serve the designs of mad and aggressive sectional ambition. They feel that the strength of the Nation in numbers, wealth, and intelligence is with them, and they are disposed to exert it, not for the North, or for the South, but for the country. Southern politicians have used the Democratic party as an instrument to carry out their insane scheme of governing the great North for exclusive Southern purposes. They succeeded for a time, because of Northern apathy and consciousness of strength, but they have gone too far. They have disgusted the Democratic party, which is leaving them by thousands,—leaving *them*, the Southern politicians, not the South, its rights, or its true interests.

The excesses of Southern politicians have also stimulated, encouraged, and inflamed into enthusiasm the Abolitionists, strengthened their cause, added to their numbers, and put weapons in their hands, which they know how to use with skill and effect, and are using. The wicked and reckless passions of partisan and sectional strife kindled a blaze in Kansas not yet extinguished. A burning flame from that fire was wafted so far as Harper's Ferry. When and where the wild wind of fanatic fury may take another, no one can say. All will agree, however, that the sooner the fire is quite put out the better. All will agree that it would be insane folly to kindle another.

It thus appears that the two enemies of the security of Southern society, of the interests founded on Southern industry, and of the Union, which is the protecting bulwark of both, are Southern politicians and Northern Abolitionists. The whole power and strength of the latter comes from the former. Do these politicians and the Northern Democrats still in alliance with them, really represent Southern opinion? Do the educated and conservative people of the South approve of the repeal of the Missouri Compromise, of the conduct of the present and the last administration to the people of Kansas, of the doctrine that Slavery exists by law in the Territories independent of the wishes of their people or of the power of Congress, of filibustering expeditions to extend the area of slavery, and of the Dred Scott decision, by which a slave is made mere property, and the relation between him and his master pure ownership,—the relation not of a man to a man, but of a man to a thing? Are these the principles of the Southern people? If so, they and we do not "live under the dome of the same idea." A deep gulf lies between their moral state and ours, and an "irrepressible conflict" already exists between Southern weakness and Northern strength, representative of another irrepressible conflict, never ending and still beginning, the eternal war between truth and falsehood, between right and wrong. If this be so, cotton yarn, strong as it is, cannot long hold us together.

But if the Southern people are content with the security

of Slavery as a "domestic institution," guaranteed by Northern power; if they are content with the right under the Constitution, to extend Slavery into any Territory to which it is suited by the conditions of soil and climate; if they are content with their four millions of negroes, without African importations to barbarize and degrade still more the industry of one-half the Nation, and increase the danger of servile war; if they are content to owe allegiance, not to the South, but to the Union, to promote and share in Northern prosperity, and to live with the Northern people, as one nation under one government, bound together by duty and interest, and common happiness, hopes, and destiny, to a common country, then there is a Northern party ready to meet them. There is solid ground of principle on which both can stand, and the two together may set Democrats and Abolitionists at defiance.

This is a long preface to a short book, but not too long for the occasion, if what it contains be true. To the Northern and Southern conservative party, yet to be organized, but whose union, there is reason to hope, is preparing in the minds and hearts of the people, this little volume is addressed. The fanatics of Slavery, and the fanatics of Anti-slavery, are beyond the pale of argument.

November 12th, 1859.

THE LAW

OF THE

TERRITORIES.

THE TERRITORIES AND THE CONSTITUTION.

"Houses are built by rule and Commonwealths."

HERBERT.

THE wily and witty Talleyrand was once asked the meaning of the word non-intervention, so often used in European diplomacy. "It is a word," he replied, "metaphysical and political, not accurately defined, but which means much the same thing as intervention." The same word has been frequently employed, of late years, in our politics, with the same difference between its professed and its practical signification. It was introduced for the first time in reference to the government of the Territories, when it became an object for the South to gain

Kansas as a slave State. Two obstacles were to be overcome. One was the Missouri Compromise, which was a solemn compact between North and South to settle a disturbing and dangerous question; the other was, a possible majority in Congress that, it was feared, might prohibit slavery in the new territory. Southern politicians had, at the time, control of the Government, and they got rid of both difficulties by repealing the Missouri Compromise in the Kansas and Nebraska Bill. By necessary implication arising from the relation of the Territories to the rest of the nation, by the language of the Constitution, and by the uniform construction of it and practice under it from the earliest period of our history, the Territories had been subjected to the absolute control of the General Government. By the Kansas and Nebraska Bill they were withdrawn from that control. The principle of popular sovereignty, it was said, applied to them as well as to the States, and this bill declared that the people of the Territories should be perfectly free to choose their own domestic institutions and regulate their own affairs in their own way. Non-intervention by Congress was loudly proclaimed by all party-men and party-organs as the constitutional right of the Territories. Kansas, it was thought, would be speedily settled by Southern men, who would, of course, choose slavery as one of their domestic institutions, which would thenceforth be safe from Northern majorities in Congress.

The result, however, was different. Nature intended Kansas not for slavery but for free labor. Its temperate climate and fertile soil fit it for Saxon enterprise and industry, for the home of the dominant race, which is carrying liberty, the arts, the literature and science of civilization wherever, on this continent, that race can live and work. Kansas is not fitted for the Negro. As soon as its rich lands were opened to emigration, they attracted crowds of bold and hardy men from the North, who went there to build up homes and fortunes for themselves and their children; who brought with them love of freedom, aversion to slavery, and the fixed determination that this fine Territory should, in fact, belong to them and their children, and be cultivated by them and for them, and not by and for the Negro. Then commenced a struggle which forms a very deplorable and mortifying portion of our history—a struggle between the North and South to get possession of this Territory, not so much for the sake of its wealth as its votes. It was a political contest, and its object was power; party power, sectional power. As soon as it became apparent that the majority of the settlers were opposed to slavery, preparations were made to defeat them at the elections. Armed bands from Missouri invaded the hustings and deposited their own votes. Blood was shed. Sentinel guards were stationed on the routes leading to the disputed Territory, to keep away all emigrants from the North, and every species of fraud and violence resorted to, to secure a legislature favorable to the wishes of the South. These measures were successful. A legislature was elected by Missouri votes, and it immediately passed such laws to establish slavery, as shocked even its advocates; laws abolishing the civil rights of American citizens for the sake of holding the Negro in bondage; laws contradicting every principle of American or English liberty for the sake of sectional and party victory. A melancholy fact, full of gloomy meaning; for what security do our institutions and our doctrines inherited from the past afford, when such things can be done, and receive the sanction and support of public men and powerful parties?

This victory achieved, Southern politicians and Northern Democrats soon showed the meaning they attached to the principle of non-intervention and popular sovereignty announced in the Kansas and

Nebraska Bill, and ostentatiously paraded in messages, Congressional speeches, stump oratory, and the partisan press. The Legislature of Kansas, though proved to have been elected by fraud and violence, and by Missouri votes, was recognized as legal and valid by Congress and the President; its infamous laws were adopted and enforced by military power; the whole weight of Executive influence, in and out of the Territory, was exerted to defeat the known wishes of its people, and these efforts were continued until, at length, they culminated in the attempt to force upon Kansas the hated Lecompton Constitution, which introduced slavery against the wishes and earnest protest of nine-tenths of its inhabitants. Such was the practical application of the new doctrines of the Kansas and Nebraska Bill, made by its authors and advocates.

But this scheme did not succeed in the end. It was a struggle against physical laws which destine all such regions as Kansas for free labor, and emigrants from the North poured into the Territory in spite of border ruffians, partisan intrigue, and Presidential power. It was a struggle also against the force of an idea, so rooted in the American mind as to be a feeling or instinct rather than a political doctrine,—the idea that all government is unjust and oppressive which violates the opinions and sentiments of the governed.

Two great facts were plainly visible through the flimsy web of attorney logic and quibbling technicality, not very ingeniously woven to conceal them. One of these facts was that the people of Kansas were heartily and almost unanimously averse to slavery; the other was that the Government was trying by every means in its power to impose slavery upon them. This violation by Democrats of the fundamental principle of Democracy, aroused the nation. It was too gross even for the South, and was opposed by some of its most eminent statesmen. It excited general indignation in the North and thinned the ranks of the Democracy. The popular sentiment made itself felt in a way that could not be misunderstood or disregarded, and the Lecompton Constitution was virtually rejected by Congress, by the votes of Southern men and of Democrats, in spite of threats, denunciation, Executive patronage, and all other arts by which power seeks to maintain its abuses, and parties secure the fidelity of adherents.

It was clear, therefore, that the principle of popular sovereignty in the Territories, introduced by the Kansas and Nebraska Bill, a principle before unknown to the law and practice of our Government, would not suit the South. It appeared too probable that not only the people to inhabit all the territory north of 36·30, the old Missouri Compromise line, but also much territory south of it, would, like the people of Kansas, reject slavery if left to regulate their domestic institutions in their own way. What then were Southern politicians to do? Invoke the ancient and long-exercised, but now denied and derided power of Congress over the Territories? This might prove a dangerous weapon in the hands of possible future Northern majorities, when the question arose as to Southern territory possessed and to be acquired. It was obviously necessary to withdraw slavery alike from the control of Congress and of the people of a Territory. Some ingenuity was required for this. The Kansas and Nebraska Bill declares that the Constitution extends to the Territories. This was not an entirely new doctrine. It had been broached before by Mr. Calhoun, and insidious attempts had been made to introduce it, but were always defeated on the ground that the Constitution, by its language and the practice under it, was made for States only, and that the Territories were subject to the supreme control of Congress,—a control that had frequently been exercised, not only independently of the Constitution, but in a manner incompatible with it. Nevertheless, this doctrine was introduced, with other innovations, into the Kansas and Nebraska Bill. After the passage of that bill, the views of the South were enlarged; its novel principles of constitutional law sanctioned, and its plans of future action confirmed by the decision of the Supreme Court in the case of Dred Scott. According to that decision, the Constitution recognizes slavery as a national institution. It recognizes slaves as property; nay, as mere property, differing in no respect from other merchandise. The Territories belong to the nation. Every citizen has equal rights to them and in them. Why, therefore, may not a Southern man, as well as a Northern man, go into them with his *property?* What right has Congress to discriminate between North and South, and place one under an ignominious ban of restriction? What right have the people of a Territory to exclude their fellow-citizens from advantages enjoyed by themselves, or to undertake to decide for others what is and what is not property? The Constitution declares that slaves are property; that all the States and the people have equal rights. The Territories belong to all. Therefore, under the Constitution they should be enjoyed by all.

By this ingenious logic, the Kansas and Nebraska

Bill is made to contradict itself. It first declares that the Constitution extends to the Territories; in other words, according to the doctrines of the framers of the bill, slavery exists in them by force of the Constitution, without reference to the will of the people. It then says that the people of the Territories shall be "perfectly free to form and regulate their domestic institutions in their own way." In this manner, though by a flat contradiction of all the principles they had loudly proclaimed before, Southern politicians got rid of the power of the people of a Territory, as well as of Congress, over slavery. Slavery, they say, exists and has always existed in all the Territories independently of their people, or of Congress. Neither Congress nor the people put it in, nor can they take it out. All legislation by Congress, therefore, on this subject, from the Act of 1789, prohibiting slavery in the Northwest Territory, down to the Missouri Compromise in 1820, was unconstitutional and is void. Accordingly, the Missouri Compromise was repealed, slavery now exists in all the Territories by virtue of the Constitution, and will remain in them, under its protection, safe from Abolitionists, safe from Congress, safe even from the people of the Territories, notwithstanding the promises of the Kansas and Nebraska Bill.

But snares and perils beset the path of those who depart from truth, or from well-settled principles of law. Error, when logically carried out to its consequences, leads always to difficulty and embarrassment. It was soon discovered that this new scheme of Southern doctrine and policy would not work. Slavery is protected in the Territories by the Constitution, but what is the Constitution? It is the written plan of the Government, by which power is distributed among its departments and duties assigned to each. It is a declaration by the people of the general principles on which the Government is founded, and of the means by which those principles are to be protected and applied. But the Constitution does not execute itself. It contemplates and requires action by the powers it has ordained, to call into life and apply its principles. This is done by means of laws. The Constitution provides for the election of a President, but no President can be elected unless Congress passes laws for the purpose. It provides for the imposition of taxes, but without revenue laws no taxes can be collected. It provides for the capture of fugitive slaves, but without laws to carry this provision into effect it would be inoperative, and so in all other cases, the principles of the Constitution are latent powers which can have effect only by means of laws passed by Congress. Of what practical use, then, is this new doctrine that the Constitution extends to Territories and carries slavery along with it, unless either the Territorial Legislature or Congress make laws to carry into effect this principle; laws to enable the master to hold his slaves in bondage, and to compel their services. Such laws are necessary in the States. They are equally necessary in the Territories. No such laws are in the Constitution.

Here, then, was a new difficulty. With infinite effort of logical subtlety and partisan management, slavery had been withdrawn both from the power of Congress and of the people of the Territories, and committed to the care of the Constitution, when behold, the Constitution proves to be no protection at all. It is absolutely powerless and a dead letter, unless life be given to it either by Congress or the Territorial Legislature. But both may refuse to act. They may carry out the principle of non-intervention, so imperiously demanded by the South, and do nothing, leaving slavery to the Constitution alone. Slavery, then, is in the Territory theoretically; yet, practically, there can be no slaves, for there are no laws by which a master can control a slave. The moment one is brought into a Territory he is free.

In this dilemma Southern politicians have boldly invented and proclaimed another new doctrine of constitutional law. Congress is bound, they tell us, to make laws for the protection of slavery in the Territories. Slavery is in the Territories by the Constitution, and it is the duty of Congress to execute the Constitution. Slaves are property, made so by the Constitution, and the first obligation of Government is to protect the property of its citizens. The South is thus obliged to eat its own words, and flatly to contradict every one of those principles, to maintain which it has embroiled the country for so many years, and sown so widely the seeds of sectional strife. Its politicians are forced to invoke the authority of Congress over slavery, though they denied and attempted to abolish that authority by the Kansas and Nebraska Bill; they are obliged to deny the power of the people of a Territory, though they asserted that power in the same bill. The people, they now say, have no power over their domestic institutions, but Congress is supreme, and may impose slavery on a Territory in defiance of its wishes or its votes.

It is not easy to see, however, in what way this

new doctrine is to help the South, unless it can be sure always of a majority in Congress. New principles of law, especially when they overturn old usage and well-settled opinions, do not meet with ready assent. The power of Congress over the Territories is no doubt supreme, and has heretofore been exerted on many occasions, both to prohibit and to permit slavery. It is the right of Congress to do either, so at least we are taught by precedent and the authority of wise men in times past. No new dogma, invented to serve a purpose, can impose a new obligation on Congress or obtain universal consent. Should it turn out that any future Congress shall refuse to act in the matter at all, according to one Southern doctrine, or leave slavery to the Territorial Legislature according to another, what remedy has the South? What authority can it invoke to coerce Congress? To what tribunal can it apply for a writ of mandamus to compel Congress to perform its alleged duty? To impose a duty without a penalty and without power to enforce performance, is a nullity. Such, however, is the new doctrine unblushingly announced by Southern politicians and their Northern adherents, though it contradicts every line of the Kansas and Nebraska Bill, and is a flat denial of all the opinions for which they have contended during the last three years of political agitation and sectional hostility, created by those opinions.

Consistency is a virtue both in men and parties and governments. Without it they can inspire neither confidence nor respect. Conduct must be guided, either by principles, or by selfishness without regard to principles. To assert one opinion to-day to serve a purpose, and, when that fails, to advocate an opposite opinion to-morrow, is to add falsehood to selfishness. It would be more honest to confess the selfishness as the sole rule of action. When principles are supported and abandoned by a political party to suit emergencies, when they are not regarded as guides applicable in all times and to all cases, but as mere weapons of party warfare, employed not because they are just and true, but because they can attract adherents, cement alliances, and conciliate interests, then party questions are withdrawn from the pale of argument, and must be decided by mere force of votes. In such a contest, selfish passions reign unchecked, reason is silenced, violence and corruption contend together, until at length moral anarchy, the frightful rule of no rule, arises, which leads directly to civil and social anarchy. Southern politicians, aided by Northern Democrats, repealed the Constitution and overturned the practice of the Government settled by the experience of sixty years and sanctioned by the conduct and opinion of the wisest and best men of our country. They introduced a new doctrine and a new law, and now, when that doctrine and law are found unfit instruments for their purpose, they abandon both and proclaim another principle inconsistent alike with those they have thrown aside, and with the Constitution they have violated. Is it not fair to conclude that Constitution and laws and principles are to them mere tools with which they hope to accomplish their objects. That they have one purpose only and guide in all their action,—to gain power for slavery and the South. That all principles are to them alike, provided they serve this purpose; that none are false and none true, none just or unjust, but all are these by turns and all are welcome, if they serve the present need. Such a party can never be overcome by argument, for its object is not truth, but success. It abandons all the principles for which it contended, without hesitation, the moment they become useless, thus acknowledging their falsehood, and adopts another set, equally false, for which it contends as zealously as it did for the first. It is equally insincere in both. It is sincere only in one thing,—the attainment of its ends. Such a party is very dangerous, for should its ends be unreasonable or unattainable, neither the law nor policy of the country can ever be settled on a firm and durable basis. When no principle is considered too well established to be questioned, and no compact so solemn that it may not be broken, and when the object of discussion is agitation, and, by means of agitation, victory, how is it possible that a subject so difficult and exciting as slavery can be withdrawn from the contests of party and placed on secure foundations. Nothing is secure but what is true, and truth, not always to be got by seeking, is sure to be missed when not the object of search.

But these abuses fortunately, in most cases, work their own cure. Power under a free government, leaves a party that habitually disregards the obligations of truth and justice. The mere selfish pursuit of interest by one side, induces the same course by the other in self-defence, and this is not government but war, the last resort when argument and reason fail. The law is the protection of all, and a party that violates the law, to accomplish ambitious designs, attacks the security of all. The Southern party has gone much too far. Elated by success and power, it has become aggressive. It has removed ancient landmarks, it has introduced new and false doctrines into our law, it has at length abandoned all principle whatever, and stands forth the avowed champion of Southern interests only, declaring that it will either rule the Union or break the Union. It is difficult to believe that this party really represents the enlightened opinion of the South, or will be sustained by it. Unless public sentiment be hopelessly corrupted, moderate men abandon extreme ideas when strife reaches a certain point of exasperation, invoke the influence of patriotic feeling and try to find some principles, just for all and in which all can agree, to restore harmony and united action for the common good. Indications are not wanting to show that many in the South are revolted by the monstrous doctrines and exorbitant demands of Southern politicians. They see in them neither truth, nor justice, nor safety. Neither do they see these in the opinions and schemes of Northern Abolitionists. Between the two extremes they would gladly find a path of safety, and so also would the great body of the Northern people. The South has lived and grown in wealth and strength under the Constitution and the laws made by its founders. They were made for its protection, and they have protected it. They were made for the happiness and security of the whole country, and they have promoted these in ample measure. It would be strange indeed, if the time has now arrived when the safety of the South demands that this Constitution be repealed, that these laws be declared null and void, as founded in error or injustice, or behind the age in which we live. Southern politicians have hastily and rashly decided this question. Perhaps they made a mistake. If it can be shown that the Constitution is still sufficient for the protection of Southern interests, that the laws passed by the men who watched over the infancy of the Government were just to the South, and are so still, the decision of these politicians may possibly be reversed by the Southern people.

Slavery is a very different thing now from what it was sixty years ago. It has grown with the growth of the country into proportions far greater than were dreamed of in the philosophy of the founders of the Government. They looked forward to the time when it could with safety and advantage be abolished. They did not foresee that the number of slaves would increase to four millions, and the products of their labor become the basis of the commerce and manufactures of the world. Slavery no longer means the ignorant, indolent, expensive labor of a barbarous race, brought by rapine from their native land, unjustly held in bondage here, a moral, social, and economical evil, to be got rid of as soon as possible by emancipation or colonization or amalgamation, and the labor of the free white race substituted in its stead. The times have changed since there were seven hundred thousand slaves in the South, worth from one hundred to two hundred dollars each, and since the creation of the cotton crop. Slavery now means the industry of one-half the nation. It means Northern commerce and manufactures, Northern cities, Northern wealth and progress. It means rice, sugar, tobacco, cotton; commodities that enter every household in the civilized world, and constitute, in a greater or less degree, the necessaries, comforts, and luxuries of all nations. Slavery means also security to Southern society, safety to their homes, peace, and order. It means, too, countless wealth, present and prospective, in the slaves themselves, regarded as property, and in the produce of their labor, now so great, and which commerce requires in larger quantities every year to supply a demand which increases with the progress of the world in civilization and the arts. Slavery has, therefore, a meaning which it had not in 1789 or in 1820. It has become indissolubly connected with great interests; it carries with it the fortunes of a mighty future. It has moral, social, political influences, of terrible significance. The Negro has laid a grasp of iron on the country which cannot be shaken off. Four millions of men, constituting and producing hundreds of millions of wealth, and influencing all other wealth, is a commanding fact in the economy of the nation. Four millions of an alien race, with spiritual life in them, with passions and affections; a race forever rooted in our soil, and growing as fast as we grow, to be kept in subjection, and governed for their good and ours, is another commanding fact, imposing on us duties and responsibilities, not without risk. The Act of 1789 was a Southern measure, so was the Missouri Compromise. Both were approved by Southern men, and could not have been passed without their consent. Both were acts of Congress, and are repealable by Congress. A change of circumstances necessarily leads to a change of counsels. Since those acts were passed, slavery has altered. Is it surprising that the opinions and purposes of Southern men should alter with it? Slavery has now an importance, compared with which, in 1789, or even in 1820, it was insignificant. It has also a future then unsuspected, but now clearly revealed, opening vast vistas of power and wealth, of difficulty and danger. Is it not the part of wisdom for those who are the masters of that wealth, for whom and whose children slavery is a fate, to which they are bound, for good or for evil, by chains stronger than the fetters of the slave himself; is it not their duty to protect that great present, to provide for that greater future?

Let us treat this subject with large and liberal views, with impartial and candid judgment. It is too big a thing for petty quibbling or technical argument, or narrow sectional or partisan intrigues and management. The prosperity and safety of the South concern the Nation. They involve the Union, and with it the happiness now and forever of the whole people. The question is, Does the Constitution, as heretofore understood and construed, afford protection and all reasonable scope and advantage to the South in the altered condition of slavery now? It was intended to give such protection. Has it failed? The question is worth considering.

All governments are modified by time and changing circumstances, and happy is that country where political innovations are like those of time or the changes of the seasons, gradual and easy, not sudden and violent like the convulsions of Nature,—the earthquake or the tornado. Government must represent the opinions of the day and meet its wants. But the present of a Nation contains a portion of the past and of the future. It combines among its people old age, manhood, and childhood. Its loosening hold never entirely quits the previous age and never completely grasps the coming, and to-day is a moving point that scarcely divides the two. Government, therefore, to be really representative of a progressive people, should yield slowly to new ideas, but it should yield; holding to what is good in the past, accepting with caution the offerings and promises of the future.

It is this reverence for age, for custom and prescription, this tough pliability, this thoughtful deliberation over novelties, and somewhat stubborn resistance to change, that constitutes much of the excellence of that noble growth of time, the English Constitution. It has changed, but has been conservative in its changes, and resembles those ancient rural castles that still remain in the island, where are to be seen, blended in one harmonious whole, the towers and donjon-keep of feudality, the baron's hall of Queen Bess, and the modern drawing-room, filled with the latest inventions of Parisian upholstery; armor worn by the Crusaders, portraits by Van Dyke and Reynolds, and landscapes by Turner; a park, shaded by oaks, the growth of centuries, surrounding French flower-gardens, the creation of the last year. There is great difference between the politics of England and the action of its Government under Elizabeth and under Victoria, yet King, Lords, and Commons still remain; and the Englishman to-day appeals to Magna Charta, the Petition of Right, and the Bill of Rights, just as he did in 1215, in 1645, and 1688.

These great organic acts of Government, together with usage and precedent, form the unwritten Constitution of England. They were merely declaratory of principles already established in the opinions of the people, and revered by them as safeguards of rights they had inherited. The principles remain, the rights remain, much of the outside form remains, and what of the last has changed has slowly changed, as portions became unfit to meet new wants and new ideas. In like manner our Constitution was a formal declaration of the principles held as true and just by those who made it, and which they also inherited. The Constitution created nothing except forms and an apparatus of Government, to give life, and force, and security, to those principles. It could create nothing else. A Constitution that invested with power any principles other than those which lived in the minds and hearts of the people, would be a nullity,—could not, indeed, have been made. Those principles are still alive. Nothing has been added to them, nothing taken away, nothing has weakened them since the Constitution was formed. If its shield was broad enough to cover them then, it is broad enough now.

The spirit of our Constitution was republican. A republic suited the existing condition of our people, and therefore they demanded one. Anything but the principles of a republic embodied in the Constitution would not have satisfied their wishes, or been in harmony with their opinions, and could have been imposed on them only by physical force. This Government, therefore, is a republic, formed by a union of republican States. It so happened that in some of those States, slavery existed when they met together to create a union. Slavery was a part of their domestic and civil policy, deemed by them essential to their prosperity and safety. It was clear, therefore, that the new Constitution must contain slavery and republicanism too, must give life and protection to both, otherwise these States could never accept it. Therefore, although some of the

States were no friends or approvers of slavery, this protection was granted, not as a favor, but a right; not grudgingly, but fully and completely. It was not yielded, but admitted as the just claim of equals and brothers, engaged together in the noble work of building up an empire of political liberty for the great Saxon race, whose destiny it was to inherit, and subdue, and cultivate, and adorn, a vast continent; whose energy and intellect were to fill its wide borders with the arts and knowledge of civilization, and who should be bound together by the same laws and institutions, and by the stronger ties of common principles, interests, hopes, and loyal love of country, so that the jealousies and animosities which made Europe a battle-field, might never have place among them.

Now one principle of republican Government is equality before the law. Not equality of condition or property,—a power stronger than republicanism prohibits that,—but equality of rights. The circumstances attending the formation of the Union, gave peculiar prominence to this principle, for it was of necessity to be applied not to citizens only, but to States. Accordingly we find the equality of both amply provided for by the Constitution. In the eye of this great organic law, the States are equal, and the citizens are equal; nay, the people of each State have the privileges of citizens in every other State, so anxious were the founders to obliterate differences, and to weld all parts into a harmonious whole.

We have then a Government made by slave States and free States, acting together as equals, who formed a Constitution which asserted and provided for their equality, and at the same time recognized slavery and gave it protection. Is it unreasonable, therefore, that equality should be claimed by the people of the slave States? Is it not true that they have the same rights as the people of the North in the Territories, which are national property, and that these rights are violated, that the great principle of equality before the law is violated, if they should be excluded from this domain, which is theirs as well as ours? It may be said that Congress has, on various occasions, prohibited slavery in the Territories. True, but with the consent and co-operation of the Southern States. Without that consent it could not have been done. Slavery has changed in its scope and magnitude, its tendencies and prospects. When Southern men consented to its prohibition, they hoped and believed that the time would come when it could be abolished altogether. Cotton and commerce have altered their views. They now seek to cherish slavery, and to extend it. They see in it the sources of wealth, and power, and progress. The markets of the world demand from them products which slavery only can supply. Negro labor is the key that unlocks for them the treasures of all nations, which prevents their own land from becoming a wilderness again; and negro labor, in the present state of Southern society, means slavery. They therefore value it as we value our grain fields, our coal and iron, and are determined to keep it. They have as much right to these as to their former opinions, and to have them represented in the Government. Congress has plenary power over the Territories, often exercised on this subject of slavery; but should Congress exercise its power to the injury of the Southern people, should it make a distinction between them and the North in regard to the national domain, then the great republican principle of equality before the law would be violated. Southern politicians have not strengthened, but greatly damaged their cause, by introducing the false and wicked dogma that slaves are mere property,—not men, but things; that the relation of master to slave is the relation of man to merchandise, not of man to man; that the master has no duties, the slave no rights, and exists not for his own happiness, but wholly for the mercenary benefit of his owner. This detestable doctrine, contradicted by philosophy, by religion, by morals, and by the general sentiment and practice of the South, is at once unnecessary and odious. It revolts the moral feeling of the world, and is of no use in the argument. The truth is sufficient. To mix falsehood with it weakens its force. Slavery is sanctioned by the Constitution. The people of all the States have equal rights in the Territories. To exclude the people of the slave States therefore, *without their consent*, would be unequal and opposed to the spirit and intent of the Constitution. This, however, is what Congress has never yet done.

There is another principle of republicanism embodied in the Constitution, important as the first, and as dear to those who framed it, and to the American people of the present time. That principle is, that all just and free government must be founded on the consent of the governed. On their consent, not necessarily on their votes. Votes are merely one means of expressing consent. This principle is the very vital essence of republican liberty. The Constitution meant to assert and establish it, if it meant anything. The whole structure of the Government was planned for the purpose of subjecting power to the will of the people, of making all authority representative and responsible. Congress has supreme power over the Territories, and must have, because of their relations to the Government. But this power is not arbitrary and despotic. Though unchecked by the provisions and language of the Constitution, it is not therefore lawless, to be exercised without the guidance of constitutional principles. Is there nothing but the letter of the law? Do American citizens cease to have rights when they step from a State into a Territory, and is their government on one side of a dividing line a Republic, and on the other side a despotism, or do they carry with them the living principles of the Constitution wherever they dwell under the flag of their country? They do not take with them the laws of the States, nor any laws except those given to them by Congress. They cannot go into the Territories at all, nor own an acre of land in them, nor form a Territorial Government, nor make a State Constitution, nor be admitted as a State, without the consent of Congress. But they take the principles of American liberty, and if they live solely under the control of the General Government, that Government is a Republic, and bound to use its authority in a republican manner. Republicanism is the law of its being, all its powers are trust powers, and it is a trustee for all who live beneath its sway.

What then is the rule of conduct, the unwritten law, sacred as if written in the Constitution itself, that should guide Congress in the exercise of its power over a Territory? Is it the will of the North or the South, of the majority of to-day, or to-morrow, or is it the interests, the wants, and the wishes of the people of the Territory? Because Congress has the legal control of the Territories, are they to be used as the foot-balls of parties, as mere instruments and weapons in their strife, the property of the faction that may happen for the time to have the control of Congress? Have the people of the Territories no rights because they have no votes, and is there no power but that of the ballot-box? The Territories are to become States. Their people were American citizens before they went into them, and are to become American citizens again. During the interval do they cease to be Americans? Did they leave behind them in the States their civil rights and the principles of American liberty, and among these the most important and most cherished of all, the right of expressing their wishes to their own Government, and of having those wishes respected? Their wishes. The wishes of the people of the Territory, honestly and fairly ascertained and deliberately expressed, not the passions or plans of the North or the South, or of one or the other political party. Congress is not the agent or delegate or representative of the Territories, but their guardian. During their inchoate, immature condition, the rude settlers are deficient in knowledge and capacity for self-government, which come with wealth and numbers and social progress. They are not fit to be trusted wholly with their own guidance or the destinies of the future State. As they advance, however, in population, their opinions are entitled to more consideration, and a Territorial Government is provided to be the organ of those opinions. The power of Congress over the Territories has been likened to that of a parent over a child. Is not this power governed by duty and responsibility? Is a father bound to regard the welfare of his child, or the interests and designs of some other party? Are the inclinations of his child, as he advances to maturity, in reference to his plans of life, to the choice of a business or profession, entitled to no respect, or is the father to have no guide but his own arbitrary, perhaps ignorant and prejudiced will? All power is trust power. There is no such thing known to ethics as power without duty and responsibility. The power of Congress over the Territories is coupled with the duty of exerting it solely for their good in a republican spirit, because that is the vital, organic spirit of Congress itself, of the whole framework of the Government created by the Constitution.

It has been said that the Constitution was made for the States, not for the Territories. That its provisions apply therefore only to the States, and the power of Congress over the Territories, not being limited and defined in the Constitution, is therefore unlimited and supreme. This is true, but it does not follow that Congress may rightfully disregard the fundamental principles of liberty which the Constitution was intended to establish and protect; and though its language, and checks, and limitations, do not extend to the Territories, its spirit and intention do. There is a distinction, very obvious, though lost sight of in the discussion of this question both by Northern and Southern politicians, between the rightful possession of power and the exercise of it. Legal power may be unjustly and oppressively used. Constitutional power may be unconstitutionally used, and is so, when constitutional principles, or the settled construction of those principles, are violated, though the injured party may have no legal redress, save an appeal to the ballot-boxes of the nation. According to the theory of the British Constitution, Parliament is omnipotent. This and the maxim that the King can do no wrong, mean merely that there is no positive law to limit the power of Parliament, or to punish the King for crime. Yet the authority both of Parliament and the Crown is bounded and controlled by well-settled principles and rules, sanctioned by time and the custom of ages, and the rights and liberties of England are safe as if those principles were defined in a formal document, and will be safe so long as love of liberty and reverence for right, live in the hearts of the English people. Among these rights, none is held by them more sacred, though they do not use the ballot-box, than the right of self-government. This is the right of all Englishmen, at home and abroad, wherever the jurisdiction of their Government extends. Mr. Burke, the most eloquent and profound writer on the British Constitution, whose opinions, too, were emphatically opposed to democratic theories, asserts it, even when speaking of the revolted Colonies of North America, over whom the authority of Parliament was surely as complete as that of Congress over the Territories. In his letter to the sheriffs of Bristol he says: "When I first came into a public trust, I found

Parliament in possession of unlimited power over the Colonies. I could not open the statute book, without seeing the actual exercise of it, more or less. . . . I had very earnest wishes to keep the whole body of this authority perfect and entire as I found it, not for our own advantage only, but principally for the sake of those *on whose account all just authority exists ; I mean the people governed.* . . . . No legislative rights can be exercised, *without regard to the general opinions of those who are to be governed.* . . . In effect to follow, not to force the public inclination ; to give a direction, a form, a technical dress, and a specific sanction to the *general sense of the community*, is the true end of legislation." Such was the language of this philosophic statesman as to the rights of English subjects in American Colonies. Are the rights of American citizens in American Territories less worthy of respect?

Slavery exists in many States of this Union by virtue of their laws and the sanction of the Constitution. These States have equal rights with the others to the Territories, and the people of all the States, when they go to the Territories, are subject to the power of Congress. Should a Territorial Legislature, fairly representing the people, make that the free labor of the white man suited their soil and climate, that their wish was to keep their land for their own race, and not for the Negro, to keep it free from slavery for themselves and their posterity? Would it not be a monstrous violation of the principles of republican government, should Congress reject such a demand, disregard the sober, matured, and known wishes of the people, their moral sentiment and feelings of right, their hopes and plans for themselves and their children, and attempt to force slave labor and a slave code upon them against their conscience and honest conviction? Yet this is the duty of Congress according to the last doctrine of the South. Slavery is already in the Territory, it is said, by virtue of the Constitution, and neither the people nor Congress can take it out. Nay, because slavery cannot defend itself, nor can the Constitution defend it without laws, Congress is bound to pass slave codes for the Territories, in defiance of the opinions and wishes of their people, and to enforce these codes by the military force of the nation. Such are the principles now put forth by Southern politicians, confirmed by the Supreme Court, and offered by Northern Democrats to the American people.

that the free labor of the white man suited their soil and climate, that their wish was to keep their land for their own race, and not for the Negro, to keep it free from slavery for themselves and their posterity? Would it not be a monstrous violation of the principles of republican government, should Congress reject such a demand, disregard the sober, matured, and known wishes of the people, their moral sentiment and feelings of right, their hopes and plans for themselves and their children, and attempt to force slave labor and a slave code upon them against their conscience and honest conviction? Yet this is the duty of Congress according to the last doctrine of the South. Slavery is already in the Territory, it is said, by virtue of the Constitution, and neither the people nor Congress can take it out. Nay, because slavery cannot defend itself, nor can the Constitution defend it without laws, Congress is bound to pass slave codes for the Territories, in defiance of the opinions and wishes of their people, and to enforce these codes by the military force of the nation. Such are the principles now put forth by Southern politicians, confirmed by the Supreme Court, and offered by Northern Democrats to the American people.

If Congress be the government of the Territories, its power must be exerted for the good of the people who live in them, not to serve the designs of people who do not live in them. The Territories are, for a time, placed under the guardian care of Congress for this very purpose. Under this protection the people of the States, when they go to the Territories, meet on common ground, and the two great principles of republicanism,—self-government and equality before the law,—work harmoniously together. All have an equal right to go to the Territories, to vote when there for or against slavery, to elect a Territorial Legislature, and to ask and expect from Congress laws, or the approval of laws, according to the will of the majority, fairly and honestly ascertained. This is true equality for North and South; it is the equality that the people enjoy in the States, and it is all that the law can give. It cannot give equality of power any more than it can give equality of population, on which political power depends. When it shall happen that a Territory in which there are slaves and masters, and the masters are a majority of the people, ask of Congress laws for the protection of slavery, and their petition is rejected, then the South will have reason to complain that its rights are violated. But this is a thing that Congress has not yet done.

It is satisfactory to find the truth of these principles, and the justice and wisdom of the old law, vindicated by the legislation of Congress on the subject of slavery in the Territories, from the earliest period of our history, until the new doctrines introduced by the Kansas and Nebraska Bill. The duty of Congress to exercise its power for the benefit of the people of the Territories, and with a just regard both to their wishes and to the equal rights of the States, are principles which, sound in theory, have been successfully applied in practice. They have been at times denied, and serious dangers have been caused by attempts to resist them, but principles of Government are strengthened and confirmed by the shock of conflict, if they triumph; and these have triumphed in every contest whenever opposed, from 1789, when the first Congress assembled under the Constitution, to 1854, when they were overthrown by the Kansas and Nebraska Bill; and that bill has been the prolific source of agitation and discord ever since. Before the passage of that false and fatal law, the right of Congress to legislate for the Territories on all subjects was never disputed. The only question that arose was, whether the exercise of the right was expedient and just in the particular case, and so strong were the principles of the Constitution, that they resisted every attempt to prohibit slavery in any Territory, without the consent and co-operation of the South, or against the wishes of the people of the Territory. Slavery was excluded from the Northwest Territory in 1789, in conformity to the Ordinance of 1787. This was a Southern measure, passed to execute a contract made by the Government of the Confederation with Southern States, and the prohibition of slavery was part of that contract. All the provisions of the Ordinance of 1787 were afterwards, in 1790 and 1802, extended to the Southwest Territory, *except the clause forbidding slavery*, and this exception was made because, in that Territory, slavery already existed and was likely to continue, being suited to its soil and climate. When Louisiana was acquired, in 1803, Congress assumed absolute control over it, by a bill drawn by Mr. Jefferson, and passed by Southern votes. This bill did not abolish slavery, because Louisiana was then, as now, inhabited by planters and the owners of slaves, but absolute power over the subject was claimed by Congress and exerted. Although the foreign slave-trade was then constitutionally lawful for the people of the

States, it was prohibited to the people of this Territory. No slave imported since May 1, 1798, was permitted to enter the Territory at all, the bill thus anticipating the time when the slave-trade could be prohibited to the people of the States, and showing that the public men of the period, did not consider the limitations of the Constitution applicable to the Territories. The provisions of this act were applied to the case of Florida in 1819 and 1822. In 1819, an effort was made to prohibit slavery in the Territory of Arkansas while it remained a Territory, and without reference to its future condition as a State. Arkansas was in the South, it was suited to slave labor in soil and climate, slavery existed in it and its people approved of slavery. The South opposed the restriction, and Congress rejected it. No one denied the power of Congress over the subject; on the contrary, that power was expressly asserted and admitted by Southern men during the debate. The measure was resisted wholly on the ground that it was inexpedient and unjust, both to the South and to the people of the Territory. In 1820 a bill was introduced to prohibit slavery in all Territory north of latitude 36° 30′. The Territory of Missouri was included in these limits. Its people approved of slavery, were owners of slaves, and remonstrated with earnestness against the bill. They were supported in their appeal by Southern members of Congress. After a severe and protracted contest, Missouri was excepted from the operation of the bill, and it became a law, and that law was the celebrated Missouri Compromise, passed by the votes of Southern men, approved by a Southern President, and by a cabinet, a majority of which was also from the South. Some of these men were the most eminent for talents and virtue, then in the country.

It may be said that this law was a violation of the equal rights of the Southern people, by excluding them from a large portion of the national domain. The answer is, not merely that this was done with their consent, their representatives having approved the law, but that the law did recognize their rights, by dividing between them and the Northern people all the Territory then possessed by the Government. It may also be said, that by prospectively prohibiting slavery, the possible wishes of the future inhabitants of this vast region, then for the most part a wilderness, were disregarded. But what would *probably* be their wishes was respected, and governed the selection of the line; else why not forbid slavery south of it, and leave the north open? Reason and experience both taught that the climate and soil of the North are unfit for slavery; that the Negro cannot thrive and work there, but the white man can; and, therefore, the land would be occupied by the dominant race, to the exclusion of the Negro. The law was a prediction, and the result has proved its truth. In none of the States into which the Northwest Territory has been divided, have the people ever desired to introduce slavery, and as soon as Kansas was opened, though the restriction was removed, settlers from the North filled it, as the surrounding air rushes into a vacuum. It is to be remembered, also, that the law was a compromise, and something was to be surrendered by each party. It was intended to restore peace at a time when sectional strife threatened the repose of the country and the safety of the Union, and it did restore peace. Neither as a law nor a compromise was it a fetter on the future. Should altered circumstances and changed opinions render expedient another arrangement, the law might be repealed. It has been repealed; whether wisely or not, time has already shown.

The power of Congress over slavery in the Territories was again exerted in the year 1845, when Texas was admitted into the Union. The Missouri Compromise was re-enacted. In all of Texas north of 36° 30′, slavery was prohibited; in all south of that line, slavery was permitted, if *the people should desire it.* This law was accepted by Texas, which was an independent sovereignty, annexed by compact to this country, and this compact also passed by Southern votes and was approved by a Southern Cabinet, of which Mr. Calhoun was Secretary of State. It was also emphatically approved by Mr. Buchanan, because "it went to re-establish the Missouri Compromise, by fixing a line within which slavery was in future to be confined." He declared that when that Compromise was made, he "had set his foot on the solid ground then established, and there he would let the question stand forever." Four years after, the Missouri Compromise was again sanctioned, when a Territorial government was organized for Oregon, in 1848. The result of the war with Mexico was the acquisition of a large domain from that country. It became necessary to divide this region into Territories, and to organize its people into Territorial governments. A dispute at once arose between North and South for the possession of these Territories, rivalling in violence and bitterness the contest which was closed by the Missouri Compromise of 1820. In the year 1849 an attempt was made to extend the Missouri Compromise line to the Pacific, with a provision expressly recognizing slavery south of that line; in other words, to introduce slavery, not merely where it did not exist, but where it was opposed by the habits and opinions of the inhabitants, and by the conditions of soil and climate. Now it so happened that in these Territories, California, New Mexico, and Utah, slavery was excluded by law at the time of the acquisition. Congress respected that law as an expression of the wishes of the people, and refused to legislate on the subject at all. It would not prohibit slavery, because it was already prohibited; it would not establish it, because it was not suited to the wants or wishes of the people. These reasons were embraced by Mr. Clay in the Compromise measures of 1850, in these words:

"*Resolved*, That, as slavery *does not exist by law and is not likely to be introduced* into any territory acquired by the United States from the Republic of Mexico, it is *inexpedient* to provide by law, either for its introduction into or exclusion from any part of the said territory; and that appropriate Territorial Governments ought to be established by Congress in all of the said territory, not assigned as the boundaries of the proposed State of California, without the adoption of any restriction or condition on the subject of slavery." This bill was also a compromise of the pretensions of parties, like the Missouri Compromise, for the sake of peace. It yielded no principle, but on the contrary affirmed and was founded on all those by which the legislation of the country had been guided since 1789. The power of Congress was implied by the declaration that to exercise it in the particular case was "*inexpedient.*" The present and probably future wishes and interests of the people of the Territories were respected, and, as to the equal rights of South or North, the only rights their citizens had, was to go into the Territories if they chose, and, when there, to obey the laws if they could not change them by their votes. This measure had also the merit of settling the question of slavery as to all the territory then belonging to the Government, and thus withdrawing a cause of dangerous excitement from the politics of the country.

It appears, then, that up to a period so late as 1850, the uniform practice of the Government had established the rightful power of Congress over the Territories, unlimited by any provisions of the Constitution, and had established also, that this power ought to be so exercised as not to violate the rights of the States or of the people of the Territories.

These principles have also been exemplified in the organization of the Territorial Governments. The Territories are treated as infant republics, the wards, until they attain their majority, of a mature republic; inchoate States, trusted under watchful care, until they learn how to use them, with political power and the apparatus for applying it, as children are trusted with guns and horses. They have Governors, Judges, Marshals, but these are appointed by the President, and are removable by him. They are his agents, whose duty it is to administer his authority and to advise him as to the condition of the Territory. There are Territorial Legislatures, elected by the people, but all the laws are subject to revision and repeal by Congress. They are not so much laws, therefore, as petitions, informing Congress of the needs and desires of the people. A Territory also sends a delegate to Congress, but he has no vote. His office also is to give information and to represent, not the sovereign will, but the opinions and sentiments of the people, and to explain to Congress their circumstances and interests. In all these provisions, whilst the supreme authority of Congress is asserted, ample care is taken that it may be exerted for the good of the Territory, and that those subjected to it shall have the means of making their wishes known. They have not the means of making their will obeyed, and, should they be oppressed and governed arbitrarily, not for their own benefit, but to serve the designs of other parties, they have no remedy but an appeal to the sympathy and justice and ballot-boxes of their countrymen. This appeal was made in the case of Kansas, and not in vain.

Under the old law and practice, therefore, slavery, until the year 1850, had not only been safe, but had steadily and rapidly grown in power and extent. It had grown indeed into gigantic proportions; and the law was not an iron ring, but an elastic band, like the bark of a tree, and permitted its growth. In fact, the law restrained slavery only where it was restrained by the superior laws of nature. Wherever soil and climate were adapted to it, it was free to go; it was restricted only where it could not go or could not remain. The law therefore gave to slavery all that, from its own nature, it can ever attain, the privilege of seeking a congenial home wherever, in our broad territories, it can find one. No change has taken place or ever can, in the position of slavery, to require a different law. The line of the Missouri Compromise was wisely chosen. Slavery can never go north of that line; on the contrary, from the operation of general causes, stronger than party "platforms," it is gradually receding to the south of it.

But, to possess every advantage and scope not denied by the laws of nature did not satisfy Southern politicians. In the year 1854, aided by Northern Democrats, they succeeded in passing the Kansas and Nebraska Bill, by which the well-settled principles of the Constitution, ancient usage, and a solemn compact, were alike overthrown. How cautiously, insidiously, and cunningly this bill was concocted, by what intrigues, arts, menaces, and party coercion it was introduced, and by what frauds, machinations, and tyrannical abuse of power it was passed, have been explained by Mr. Benton in his "Examination of the Dred Scott Case." These proceedings were not creditable to the South or its adherents, but to dilate upon them is apart from the purpose of this argument. The bill itself, so far as it relates to the present question, is in these words:

"The Constitution and all laws of the United States, which are not locally inapplicable, shall have the same force and effect within the said Territory of Nebraska as elsewhere in the United States, except the eighth section of the act preparatory to the admission of Missouri into the Union, approved March 6th, 1820, which, being inconsistent with the principles of non-intervention by Congress with slavery in the States and Territories, as recognized by the Legislature of 1850, commonly called the Compromise Measures, is hereby declared inoperative and void; it being the true intent and meaning of this Act, not to legislate slavery into any Territory or State, nor to exclude it therefrom, but to leave the people thereof perfectly free to form and regulate their domestic institutions in their own way, subject only to the Constitution of the United States."

The contradictions, duplicity, and absurdity of this law are obvious at once. The first sentence announces a change in the settled principles and policy of the Government, else why declare that the Constitution *shall* extend to Nebraska, if it already extended there. It and the laws of the United States are to have the same force and effect there as "*elsewhere.*" Elsewhere can only mean States, which are also put on the same footing with Territories in other parts of the bill. What provisions of the Constitution are locally inapplicable to them, the bill does not mention, but as the Constitution does not give to their people a State Government or the right

7

to vote for a President or for Congress, or subject them to taxation or provide for them a Federal Judiciary; and as all its clauses, from beginning to end, except that which invests Congress with absolute control of the soil of the Territories, apply in express terms to States, it would be difficult to find any other provision in it that does apply. Next comes the repeal of the Missouri Compromise. The reason given for this is, that it is inconsistent with the non-intervention by Congress with slavery recognized in the Compromise of 1850. But this is a manifest and most impudent falsehood, for that law declares positively, that Congress does not intervene, because in the particular case, it is "inexpedient" to do so, and gives the reason why it is inexpedient, as before stated. The power of Congress was asserted by Mr. Clay who made the law, and the terms of it were chosen for the very purpose of preventing any inference being drawn from it, against that power. The bill goes on to declare that it does not intend to "legislate slavery into any Territory or *State*, or to exclude it therefrom." The meaning of this sentence is not easy to find out. Why has the word "State" a place in it? Does it mean that if the intention of Congress were different, it has the power to meddle with slavery in the States, either to introduce it or exclude it? If Congress has no such power, how can it have any "intent" on the subject at all? Power or no power, however, Congress on this occasion does not exercise it, for the bill generously declares, that it leaves "the people thereof," that is of States as well as Territories, "perfectly free to form and regulate their *domestic institutions* in their own way." What else besides their "domestic institutions," the Territories and States are free to regulate, the bill does not say. Is slavery a domestic institution? At the time the bill was passed, slavery was so considered, and from the context is no doubt meant to be included in that term. But since then, the case of Dred Scott has been decided, by which slaves are declared to be mere merchandise. So that it is a question whether the bill would now apply to them. Marriage, however, is a "domestic institution," which, it seems, Territories as well as States may regulate in their own way, and the Territory of Utah took the liberty of doing so, even without the previous sanction of this law. It is remarkable, too, that the bill, whilst declaring the *perfect* freedom of the Territories, should still have left them subject to the power of the President, who, as before, is permitted to appoint their Governor, Judges, and Marshals, officers who are his agents, and without whose sanction, the acts of the Territorial legislature can neither become laws, nor be construed and applied nor executed. So that the will of the people may be defeated, should it happen to be opposed to the will of the President, as was seen in the case of Kansas, the very case for which this new law was intended. Why, therefore, was power given to the Territories, and the means of exercising it limited or withheld? How is it possible to put States and Territories on the same level, without giving to the latter the power of States, not merely as to self-government, but as to representation in Congress and the election of the President? The whole system by which the Territories have been heretofore held in a condition of pupilage and preparation to become States has been abolished by this law, which, nevertheless, does not make them States. They are neither States nor Territories, yet their inhabitants are Americans, their country forms, geographically, a part of the nation, and the General Government is the proprietor of their soil, may sell it or refuse to sell it. What then is their position? It would be difficult for the inventors of the new law to define it.

But the word "State" was not used without a purpose. It has a latent meaning in relation to the clause by which the Constitution is extended to the

Territories. According to modern Southern doctrines, the Constitution carries slavery along with it, and it was to fortify this doctrine that Territories are classed with States in regard to slavery. It is true that the popular sovereignty clause might defeat the plans of the South as to Northern Territory. The bill, however, was not intended only for Kansas, but for future Southern acquisitions. It was hoped and expected that the people of Kansas would accept slavery, but it was deemed certain that the people of Cuba and other Southern regions yet to be annexed would accept it. The important thing, therefore, was to get the subject beyond the control of Congress. Two years afterwards the Supreme Court gave to the South a higher ground to stand upon, and its politicians have risen in their demands. If the Dred Scott case be law, slavery is in the Territories, though there be no slaves, independent of Congress and the people, waiting the arrival of slaves, and no earthly power can take it out. Armed with this more efficient weapon, the Kansas and Nebraska Bill has become obsolete and useless to the South, like the old-fashioned musket compared with a Minie rifle, and has been thrown aside. It still remains, however, on the statute book, a feat of legislation which, for mendacity, contradictory doctrines, illogical statement, and shortsighted cunning, is disgraceful to Congress, and worthy of the scenes and practices by which its enactment was surrounded and accomplished.

By abstract reasoning and by the evidence of history, it thus appears that the principles of the Constitution and the settled practice of the Government under it, have heretofore protected slavery, and are sufficient for its protection in its present state, and for its legitimate claims. Neither these principles, therefore, nor the usage that has grown out of them, should be changed. Not by the North, because they are just and true, and the law; not by the South, for the same reasons, and because they give to it all that its people can, in reason, ask or hope for, by means of any other principles or laws which they can substitute. Nevertheless, by each one of the three parties into which the country seems likely to be divided, some or all of these principles are denied, and their symmetry as a consistent whole is mutilated and marred. The extreme Southern and Democratic party violate them all, by withdrawing slavery from the control both of Congress and of the people of the Territories. The rights of both these are thus disregarded, and the rights also of the Northern States. Their people are perpetually excluded from the equal enjoyment of the Territories, so loudly claimed by the South, for they cannot carry into them their opinions and moral convictions, which are more valuable than property. They are to find in the Territories, if Democracy and the South are to prevail, a slave code, with or without slaves, made by Congress. They are therefore to live under laws imposed on them without their consent, and which violate their sense of right. Against these laws their wishes, though unanimous, cannot prevail. The South is unjust. If its citizens have a right to take with them into the Territories their property, surely Northern men have an equal right to take with them their consciences.

The extreme Northern, or Free-soil, or Abolition party, on the other hand, is only less guilty than the first, because it only violates two of the principles of the Constitution. This party asserts the legal authority of Congress, but declares that it is the right and duty of Congress to exclude slavery forever from all the Territories, without regard to the wants, habits, condition, or wishes of their inhabitants, or to the requirements of climate and soil. According to this party, the Territories are to be governed solely to suit its own ethics, and not for the benefit, or according to the wishes of the people who live in them. The rights of these people, the rights of the South, the republican principle of equality before the law, the other republican principle that political power is trust power, to be exercised for the good and according to the opinions of the governed, are thus alike contemned.

Between these two extremes, a third party has arisen. This is the Popular Sovereignty party. According to its doctrine, the will of the people of the Territory is supreme, and wholly independent of Congress. Two important principles are thus disregarded: the rightful authority of the General Government, and the right of the people of the Territories to its just and wise use for their benefit. They have a right to this, as a child has a right to the superior judgment of his father. It is for the child's advantage to be restrained in his folly or vice,—to be guided in his ignorance; it is for his advantage, too, that his mental bias, the tendencies of his character, the exigencies of his future position in life, should be considered and provided for. The settlers of a new Territory are often rude, ignorant, and turbulent adventurers, unfit for self-government. They require restraint, as is proved by the example of Utah. They require, also, just respect to their opinions and convictions, to the hopes of their future, growing out of the conditions of soil, climate, and population, as was shown in the case of Kansas. The first was a case of lawless vice, unrebuked; the second, of just and reasonable demands tyrannically resisted. The one was a weak abandonment of power, the other an oppressive use of it; and each has borne its appropriate fruits. The Territories are entitled to the fair and honest exercise of the power intrusted to the General Government,—to Congress and the President. It was given to them for the good of the Territories, and it is their duty neither to abuse it nor to abdicate it.

We have not been told by this third party how far their doctrine of popular sovereignty extends, or whether it includes all the interests and affairs of a Territory. If it does, a Territory is an independent State, politically severed from the rest of the nation, owing to it no allegiance, entitled to no protection, and bound to it by no ties except such as are voluntary. If slavery only be included in this new doctrine, if on this subject alone the will of the people of a Territory is supreme, and on all others the will of Congress is supreme, some reason ought to be given for making slavery an exception. Why are the unity and symmetry of the system of Territorial government that has grown up under the Constitution and become consolidated by usage and experience, to be destroyed for the sake of slavery? Is it because slavery is of so grave and deep an interest to the welfare of the Territories? Why then in other matters less important are they still subjected to the power of Congress? Is it because slavery is a "domestic institution?" Why then should not the will of the people control all other domestic institutions? Is it because slaves are "mere property?" Why then not subject all other property, land included, to popular control? Is it because the subject of slavery is an exciting topic among the people of the States, —because parties and sections have seized on it as a means of agitation, in and out of Congress, dangerous to the tranquillity of the country, which can be checked only by placing the subject beyond the power of Congress and thus beyond the reach of parties? The answer is, that Congress cannot abdicate its authority on the ground of expediency. Its duty is to use its authority to overcome difficulty and danger, not to recede before them. If it may give up one power, it may give up any or all. Nor can Congress delegate its power for the same reason. Trust power from its very nature cannot be delegated. It is given to be used; and not to use it when occasion requires, is to fail in the performance of duty. To break down great principles, to set aside ancient usage, to abandon legal authority, in order to appease the contests of parties, is too great a sacrifice. No true peace can come of it, only suppressed and adjourned war. The plain duty of Congress is, to maintain its constitutional authority, and to exert it with such fairness, justice, and moderation, that all parties may be satisfied. If the time has come when this cannot be done, then the time of revolution has come; but the Government should not begin with what would be the result of a successful revolution, the abandonment of its rightful powers.

The South is sectional, and exacting, and revolutionary, in its doctrines and plans. Its public men openly avow that Southern interests are their only aim and guide, and that they owe allegiance to the South first, and to the Nation afterwards, and only so far as it serves and obeys the South. They deny protection to American industry, because its benefits, they suppose, would be greater for the North than for their own section; yet they contradict their own doctrines when, as in the case of sugar, the advantage of protection inures exclusively to themselves. They claim all the Territories for slavery, without regard to the rights or opinions of their inhabitants or of the Northern people. They demand the aid of the Nation, by diplomacy or war, to acquire new and vast regions for slavery, and failing in that, they ask, by the repeal of the neutrality laws, the privilege of making war themselves for the same purpose, without the sanction of Congress. Finally, they demand the repeal of the law prohibiting the slave-trade. Negroes are wealth, and the means of wealth, and wealth is power. When these purposes shall be accomplished, then the last demand, of which they are the preliminary steps, will be made, and that is for separation; or, rather, it will follow as a natural consequence. To build up a great, Southern, slaveholding Empire, inclosing the Gulf of Mexico, and commanding the mouth of the Mississippi, and founded on negroes, cotton, rice, sugar, and tobacco, on the richest agriculture, supporting the richest commerce in the world, with all nations for tributaries, is the ambitious dream of the South, or of an influential portion of it. Perhaps the realization of this dream may lie in the future. It may be the result toward which events are irresistibly tending, the effect of world-wide causes, of which Southern politicians and their sectional selfishness are the unconscious instruments. But the vision to see this clearly is given to few, and, meanwhile, it is for us to do the duty that lies nearest; and that duty clearly is, to maintain the Union so long as it can be maintained, to defend our national existence whilst defence is possible. We can do this only by preserving in full life and activity the Constitution and those principles of political liberty which it was made to protect and enforce. When these are destroyed, all will be lost, —wealth, power, progress, peace, and happiness.

The three parties already mentioned are sectional in their purposes and false in their doctrines. There exists, however, in the sound opinion and patriotic feeling of the great mass of the people, North and South, a party unknown to politicians or to itself, scattered everywhere, in counting-houses and workshops, in the streets of cities, in rural villages, on plantations and farms; a party that is quiet, retired, unobtrusive, defensive rather than aggressive, avoiding political activity, hating the base strife of parties and demagogues, too intent, indeed, on private aims and enjoyments, but animated by loyal and conservative public sentiment. This party is the true people, the superior mind and moral feeling of the Nation. It is inefficient because of the very qualities that make it respectable. It does not go to town meetings, nor belong to political clubs; it is not represented at party conventions, nor is it very busy at the hustings; preferring rather the pleasures of domestic life, and content with the active duties of conducting the commerce, the manufactures, and the agriculture of the nation. It seldom rouses itself until danger is imminent. When it can be fully roused it is all-powerful. It is inactive and unrecognized now, in the hurly-burly of partisan politics. Demagogues never dare to address it. The time has come when this party should arise from its apathy and confidence, and assert its rights and power. It wants organization, self-knowledge, a defined plan of principles and purposes, and a representative man. Perhaps it may want them too long.

POPULAR SOVEREIGNTY IN THE TERRITORIES.

"In this the antique and well-noted face
Of plain old form, is much disfigured."
KING JOHN.

THE practical working of a law, as of a machine, discloses the truth or error of the principles on which it is made, even to the unscientific, who cannot appreciate mere abstract reasoning. Tried by this test, the absurdity of the new doctrine of Popular Sovereignty in the Territories, introduced by the Kansas and Nebraska Bill, clearly demonstrated at the time it was passed by *a priori* argument, is now made manifest by experience. Under the law as previously settled in opinion and practice, that the Federal Government is the Government of the Territories, many States of this Union lived their Territorial life in peace and tranquillity, and at the proper time took their places in the Confederacy, without opposition or excitement, either within or without their borders. The Government of Congress, during their period of probation, sufficed for their wants, and their admission as States was effected by the same authority, without complaint on their part, and often so quietly as scarcely to attract the notice of the Nation. Whether the people were "at liberty to form and regulate their own domestic institutions in their own way" or not, it is evident they got such as they liked, for they have been satisfied.

The first case to which the new doctrine has been applied, and for which, indeed, it was specially intended, is the Territory of Kansas, and it has produced a result in direct contradiction to the vaunted principle which it professes to establish, and has created such an excitement in Kansas and throughout the country, as to threaten, the President himself says, the stability of the Union. The people, so far from being allowed to form their own institutions in their own way, have been subjected, from first to last, to a government against which they have protested, even to the point of forcible resistance. A legislature and laws were imposed on them by a foreign power; a Constitution has been framed for them by an insignificant minority, and, at this moment, the President and his party in Congress are attempting to force upon them that hated Constitution, in direct opposition to their known wishes and earnest remonstrance. This clear injustice; this monstrous inconsistency between profession and practice; this gross violation of the chief principle of American and Republican Government, has revolted the moral sentiment and aroused the indignation of the country, and given to the affairs of Kansas an interest and importance so great that they absorb the attention of Congress and the Nation, and will continue to absorb it until right be done and wrong redressed. But for these causes the very existence of Kansas would scarcely be known to the majority of the people, and its admission or rejection as a State would have passed, without attracting more attention than the routine business of the legislature. It is clear the Kansas and Nebraska Bill does not work well. Its practical result is, not liberty but oppression; not the peaceful reign of justice and law, but the rule of force and fraud, assuming the forms of law; not the sovereign will of the people, choosing and regulating their own institutions in their own way, but the tyrannical sway of a minority, and of a very small minority, imposing, with the aid of the President, upon the people, institutions which they abhor, and against which they have protested by every means in their power; by voting and by refusing to vote; by argument and by entreaty; by appeals to the justice of Congress, and by appeals to the sympathy and patriotic feeling of the whole country. They have got nothing in reply from the Government but insults, threats, and bayonets.

The cause of this is plain enough. The Kansas and Nebraska Bill is a snare, a mockery, and a lie, from end to end. Its ostentatiously paraded principle, the sovereignty of the people, it does not carry out, but defeats. It emancipates a Territory from the government of Congress, and declares that its people shall be "*perfectly* free to form and regulate their domestic institutions in their own way." But they can do this only by means of laws, and what control can they exert over the laws, unless they have also control over the powers by means of which laws are made, construed, and enforced? How can they "form and regulate their *domestic* institutions," unless their *political* institutions are the representatives of their opinions and their will? For this the law does not provide. The executive power is one of these political institutions, yet the President appoints their Governor; the judiciary is another, yet the President appoints their Judge; the ministerial officers by which the decrees of courts are enforced is a third, yet the President appoints their Marshal. What is left to the people? Only the Legislature, upon whose proceedings the Governor has a veto, and whose laws are to be applied by a Court and executed by a Marshal appointed by a foreign power, and responsible only to that power. Not merely, therefore, is there erected in the Territory legal authority over which the people have no control, but the whole weight of official station and influence comes to them from abroad. How absurd, then, to talk about their sovereignty, when the institutions by which alone that sovereignty can be exercised, are in the hands of another power, also beyond their control. Suppose that, in the State of Pennsylvania, the President appointed our Governor, our Judges, and our Sheriffs. Would we be a sovereign and independent State, free to make our own laws and regulate our own affairs, or the subjects of the General Government,—nay, of the President alone? Yet the people of Pennsylvania have what those of a Territory have not,—a voice in the election of a President.

The Kansas and Nebraska Bill is therefore a contradiction and a fraud. It overturns constitutional law and usage, coeval with the foundation of our Government, and has not the poor merit of being consistent with itself. The Territories are withdrawn from the power of Congress, they are subjected to the power of the President. In Congress there are always two parties, and there is public debate. Over its action the opinion and sentiment of the country have immediate, hourly influence, and these are so many securities against unjust laws. The President represents, practically, one party. His counsels are or may be secret, in cases where he is independent of Congress. To gain a partisan or sectional object, he may be tempted to do things he would not venture to submit to the open discussion and free vote of the Legislature, and may therefore exert the whole force of his authority and influence in opposition to the wishes of the people of a Territory, who are subjected to his power without appeal, and are thus living, in fact, not under a republic, but a monarchy, and a monarch, too, not of their own choice. Better, surely, for them, the Government of Congress *and* the President, provided by the Constitution, with the check and balance of power this combination was intended to create, affording thus to the people the security of a Legislature before which their complaints could be heard, their cause argued, and where, should redress be denied, the justice of their demands could be made manifest, and bring to their aid the public opinion and ballot-boxes of the nation, the ultimate reliance of all, whether States or Territories.

The troubles in Kansas have been the result of this contradiction between the promise and performance of the Kansas and Nebraska Bill, which gives to the people only a Legislature subjected to a power irresponsible to them; offers them the privilege of managing their own affairs, yet imposes on them an authority large enough to interfere in all their affairs; an authority above their reach, liable to be directed by interests and designs foreign to them, and wielded by persons sent to them from abroad. Should the motives and plans of this foreign government harmonize with the wishes of the people, the new law would work smoothly enough so long as the harmony lasted. But should there be no harmony, on the contrary discord, then it cannot work well.

> "When two authorities are up,
> Neither supreme, how soon confusion
> May enter twixt the gap of both, and take
> The one by the other."

This is just what has happened in Kansas. Confusion, leagued with one authority, has taken the other and led it captive. Thus the inconsistency in the law has been reflected and represented by the disorder which has made Kansas a scene of agitation from the first moment of its existence. Falsehood of principle must always be followed by obstacles and difficulties in practice, because facts are governed by eternal truth, and from their nature obey truth and resist falsehood.

From the first, a large and constantly increasing majority of the people of Kansas have been opposed to slavery. The President has been, during all that time, desirous, not merely to protect slavery where it exists, but to extend it. The people of Kansas desired to see their land cultivated by free labor, to make their healthful and fertile country the home of the Saxon race, their own race, which they prefer to the African. The President was determined that it should be cultivated by slaves, and that the Negro also should make it his home. Hence arose, from the beginning, a contest between the President on one side, and the people of Kansas on the other. The forces of the President were, the Governor, the Judge, and the Marshal, their subordinates and official influence. Had the President really wished to carry out the Kansas and Nebraska Bill, according to its spirit and promise, by giving effect to the will of the people, he would have appointed to these offices men opposed to slavery, because the great majority of the people were opposed to slavery. But he did not do this. He selected pro-slavery men, and sent them to the scene of action. The people ought to have had on their side, even according to the lame and inadequate provision of the new law, the Legislature. But unluckily for them, at the very start, they lost even that defence. At the first election, the polls were invaded by armed bands from the neighboring slave State, who came with baggage wagons and artillery, the equipment and drill of military array. They came suddenly and unexpectedly, overpowered the settlers, usurped the ballot-box, put in their own votes, and triumphantly elected the candidates of the President and the South. They came not to reside, but to vote and return to their homes in Missouri. It was officially proved before a committee of Congress sent to investigate the facts on the spot, that at this election only one-fifth of the votes were legal and given by actual settlers. The rest were all Missouri votes. The Governor of Kansas did not abrogate the Legislature thus elected, which it was his duty to do, and which he might legally have done, for fraud and duress vitiate all transactions; but on the contrary, he recognized, approved, and used it, and so did the President. It is remarkable, also, that the President, in his late message sent with the Lecompton Constitution to Congress, makes no allusion whatever to these notorious facts, though they were in evidence before him, and form, indeed, part of the record in the case.

Behold, then, the people of Kansas deprived of *all* the means by which it was possible for them "to choose and regulate their own institutions, in their own way." The Executive, the Judiciary, and the Legislature were all in the hands of their enemies. They found themselves fettered, hand and foot. The Governor, the Judge, the Marshal, were the agents of the President and the South. The Legislature, which even the new doctrines of constitutional law introduced by the South, meant to be the representative of their will, was elected not by them, but by the people of Missouri, and represented the opinions of that people, as was speedily shown. At its first session, it proceeded to pass laws for the purpose of forcing slavery into the Territory; laws so monstrous, so iniquitous, so subversive of every principle of liberty and justice, that they drew forth indignant rebuke even from Southern Senators in Congress. Laws made for Kansas by Missouri. It was the duty of the Governor to veto those laws. He had the power, but he did not exert it; on the contrary, they were approved by the Governor, and received the sanction and support of the President, who nominated the Governor. To the infamous character of these laws the President has made no allusion in his late Message. In this fashion was it that the people were left perfectly free to choose their own institutions and regulate their affairs in their own way.

They would have been false to all the traditions and sentiments of their race and country, had they remained content and submissive under such thraldom. But they were far from being content, and they displayed a spirit not unworthy their "blood fetched from fathers of war-proof," and showed "the mettle of their pasture." They denounced the wicked fraud that had been practised upon them, the brutal violence to which they had been subjected. They remonstrated, they expressed their indignation in public meetings, through the press, in some cases by forcible resistance, and at last by calling a Convention at Topeka, that should really represent their wishes and form a Constitution for their future government.

This Convention certainly wanted the forms of law, but only the forms. In substance, in motive, in spirit and intention, it was American and Republican, whilst the Territoral Legislature was destitute of all these merits, and had nothing but form to recommend it. The people had been cheated out of their

Legislature, promised them even by the new law. Was it extraordinary that they should make, even an irregular effort, to get a Legislature that should represent, not the people of another State, but themselves? They had been told, by that same law, that they should be "perfectly free to form and regulate their domestic institutions in their own way." They adopted this "way" of choosing the Topeka Convention and the Constitution made by it and free labor, as their "institutions," because the Missourians and the President had stopped up the regular and legal way, which they would have preferred. Their conduct was not technically correct, but being a rude people, in a wilderness, they were probably not well versed in legal forms, and may be excused for mistaking the Kansas and Nebraska Bill for constitutional law. Their betters have made a similar blunder. Russian or Austrian despotism might censure them harshly, perhaps, but surely the instincts and feelings, if not the judgment, of the American people will pardon their error. In truth they displayed in this very act, the combined love of liberty and law, which, in all ages, has distinguished their race: their love of liberty, by resisting oppression; their love of law, by resisting it, with order, deliberation, and regularity. The President has described the Topeka Convention as revolutionary. Perhaps it was so, and a government that "decrees iniquity by law," must expect a revolution. The first Congress that set in this country was revolutionary, and it grew out of the very same cause that created the Topeka Convention; an attempt to enforce obedience without representation. The President could have prevented this Convention by doing justice to the people; but instead of this, he joined the Missourians. He even enrolled them as a *posse comitatus* to enforce the laws of the Territorial Legislature, arming their ferocity and excited passions with his own legal authority. The President, in his late Message, has condemned in strong language, the Topeka Convention, its acts and the people who supported it, but he has forgotten to mention any of the circumstances that go far to palliate their conduct, if indeed they do not wholly excuse it.

At this point of their history, the people of Kansas were made acquainted with another ally of the President,—the Federal army. They were told that the Legislature elected by Missouri votes was a valid Legislature, because according to legal form. That its laws must be obeyed. That the President could not go behind the legal form of that Legislature and those laws to inquire into their origin, but must sustain the one and execute the other, as he found them. Accordingly the Legislature and its laws, abhorred by the people, were forced upon them by the troops of the United States,—of that Government which demanded obedience from them, but refused them protection.

What then could the people do? If they appealed to the President, he was the agent of their enemies, and pointed to the law and his bayonets. If they appealed to Congress, they found its doors barred and bolted against them by the Kansas and Nebraska Bill. Congress had no power to meddle in the matter, they were told, because they were at perfect liberty to manage their affairs in their own way. So far as Congress was concerned, they were an independent people. Congress did not approve, indeed, of the border ruffians or the Territorial laws, neither did it of Austrian tyranny in Italy; but what of that? It had no right to interfere in either case. They must help themselves, and get out of the scrape as best they could; only, they must obey the President.

The people of Kansas thus found themselves caught in a trap; wound round and entangled in the meshes of a net of sophistry and falsehood, woven for them by the cunning craft of Southern statesmanship. They were subjected wholly to authority either foreign or usurped, or both, over which they had not the slightest control. All the government they had, came to them either from Washington or Missouri, was neither derived from them nor responsible to them, yet, so ingeniously had it been contrived, that, though to submit to it was base and slavish, to resist it would be treason and civil war. In this difficult emergency they adopted a line of conduct so temperate and prudent, and, at the same time, so honorable and firm, that it should excite the sympathy and admiration of all lovers of conservative liberty, and deserves a place in the annals of the country. They determined to be true at once to the Government which had cast them off and to themselves. They submitted to unjust power, clothed in the forms of law, out of deference to the law; they refused, by any voluntary act, to recognize or ratify that power. They gave to Cæsar what was due to Cæsar, and no more They kept to themselves what was due to their own conscience,—the right of protest, the right of refusing to say that a lie was the truth. The new Constitutional law enacted by Congress had left them and could not deprive them of at least one privilege,—the privilege of *not* voting.

Neither the South nor the President, their subtle machinations or their obedient bayonets, could oblige them to degrade the ballot-box. If they could not resist tyranny, they could at least refuse to sanction it, to fasten the yoke on their own necks, to kiss the rod of their oppressors. They resolved, therefore, that they would not vote at any election under the Territorial Legislature, because, by voting, they would impliedly acknowledge its legal authority. They have consistently adhered to that resolution through all temptations and trials, in defiance of menace, entreaty, and vituperation. Whenever they could vote without compromising this honorable position, they have voted, and thus demonstrated the insignificance of the minority which, aided by the President and Missouri, has ruled over them. They might, on one occasion at least, have obtained a victory over this minority, but they abstained, preferring truth to expediency. The question of slavery soon ceased to interest them. Nature and events had decided that question at a very early period of their history, and it had become merged, as soon as the Territorial Legislature assembled, in a far deeper and graver question, involving the great principles of law and liberty and civil rights, which the Constitution of this country was made to protect. They knew well that this question would stir the mind and heart of the Nation from their depths; that the honest feelings of the people would rise and swell responsive to their mute appeals; that the long roll of those deep waters would surely float them off from their barren rock of desolation; and they determined to wait for it, as the stranded mariner waits for the returning tide. Events are showing that they were not mistaken. The President has denounced them as disaffected rebels and as traitors to their country. History will tell a different story.

They adhered to their resolution to vote only when they could do so without giving their sanction to a fraud and a lie. The Territorial Legislature appointed an election for a Convention to frame a Constitution for the future State. They could easily have carried that election, but they refused to vote, because they would thus have recognized the spurious and hated Legislature. The Convention was thus the choice of a small minority. At this stage of the business, the President, moved by the ominous and extraordinary spectacle of a majority of the people standing aloof as silent spectators at an election, came forward with a proposition, which was eagerly hailed as a harbinger of peace. He promised that whatever Constitution the Convention made, should, before being presented to Congress, be first submitted to the people, to be accepted or rejected by them. The people then consented to vote, because they could, by rejecting the Constitution, get rid at once and forever of the Convention and its work, and the chief work that the Territorial Legislature was intended to accomplish. The Constitution was made, but it was not submitted to the people. It was offered to them in such a way that no man could vote against it. Two tickets were formed: one was "For the Constitution with Slavery;" the other, "For the Constitution without Slavery;" in either case, the Constitution. What the people of Kansas desired and expected was, an opportunity to condemn and spurn from them any Constitution made by a Convention that was the creature of a usurping and tyrannical Legislature, elected, not by them, but by Missourians. This opportunity they were promised by the President, and by the Governor appointed by the President. They cared nothing about slavery, which they well knew could never trouble them. What they did care about was, to get rid of a tyrannical Government which had been forced on them by fraud and violence. But even the question of slavery, professedly submitted, was not submitted at all. By a transparent trick, inconceivably paltry and base, it was so contrived that however they might vote, they must still sanction slavery in the Territory. Is it surprising that the people of Kansas refused to vote at such an election? That they felt they had been trifled with, cajoled, and cheated, by the President and by the Convention? When, subsequently, this same Constitution was really submitted to their votes by a Legislature elected by themselves, they gave sufficient proof of their sentiments in relation to it. They rejected it by more than ten thousand majority.

This Constitution has been presented to Congress by the President, notwithstanding his promise. He has sent it with a message urging Congress to accept it. His chief argument is, that immediately after the admission of Kansas as a State, with this Constitution, the people can abolish it, notwithstanding the provision it contains, that it shall not be altered for seven years. This doctrine is a thousand times more revolutionary than the Topeka Convention. It will be good news for the Abolitionists, who have long cherished a wild scheme of "amending," as they call it, the Constitution of the

Union on the subject of slavery. They have heard, no doubt with joy, that this can be done, at any time, by a mere majority of Congress and the people, instead of requiring, as that instrument provides, two-thirds of Congress or of the States to propose amendments, and a vote of three-fourths of the *States* to ratify the amendments when proposed. The principle announced by the President is precisely that on which Dorr, of Rhode Island, assisted by a rabble rout of followers, some years ago, undertook to overturn the government of a populous and flourishing State, under which its people had lived in peace and prosperity for more than a century. On the plea of an alleged majority (which turned out to have been fabricated), and an election unauthorized by law, he had the audacity to demand of the public officers to abdicate their power, and to deliver to him and his Jacobin club the treasury and the archives of the commonwealth. His doctrine is the same as that of French Red Republicans and English Chartists, and once established, would place every Constitution in the country, State and Federal, at the mercy of demagogues, mobs, and adepts in ballot-box manipulation. The President has given to the radical and dangerous principles of Dorr, the sanction of official authority.

He has proclaimed them as law in a formal and solemn State paper. Conservative men have not been pleased to find them in such a place, or revived at all. Fortunately, however, the dictum of the President has not yet become a decision of the Supreme Court, though after the opinion given in the case of Dred Scott, there is no knowing how soon it may assume that shape. The President advises Congress to accept the Lecompton Constitution on the ground of expediency. To impose it on the people of Kansas, against their wishes, will, he thinks, restore peace to that distracted Territory and to the whole country. But it is dangerous, as well as morally wrong, to sacrifice the true and the just for the sake of the expedient. Perhaps the President may be mistaken. The same party in Kansas and out of Kansas, who made this Constitution, will still exist to support it after it is accepted. To maintain it would secure two Senators and a triumph for the South and the Democratic party. They would not be likely to relinquish any legal advantage. They would claim, and have a right to claim, that the Constitution be obeyed; that it be altered or abolished only in the way provided by itself. They would demand, also, from the President, and with legal right, assistance to compel submission to the Constitution; and thus would the old controversy be renewed. Nor would the agitation which this subject causes throughout the country, cease. It would still be a sectional struggle. The parties would be the same, the principles the same; and it is for the sake of these principles, not for the sake of Kansas, that the people are excited. Kansas is not as yet of much material value in the country. Its population is small, its business is small. It does not contribute many dollars to enrich our trade. Not one in a thousand of the people cares much whether it be a slave State or a free State; but millions do care, most deeply, whether slavery is to be forced upon it against the wishes of its people; whether the Constitution of their country is to be repealed for the sake of slavery; whether their Government is to be used as an instrument to accomplish the schemes of sectional ambition in violation of the obligations of truth and justice. It is creditable to the people that they can be thus moved, and by such questions—by the ideal and the moral, the distant and the future; and all the more creditable, because the occasion is insignificant; for this proves that their feelings are excited only by the great principles involved. Whenever the contest is between right and wrong, these give importance to trifles, invest things valueless in themselves with a higher and nobler interest than any value could impart, and shed a lustre on any scene of action, however remote or humble.

> "Rightly to be great,
> Is not to stir without great argument;
> But greatly to find quarrel in a straw,
> When honor's at the stake."

It is worthy of remark, that the President, in offering to Congress the Lecompton Constitution, confines his censure to those who opposed it. All the crimes to which that instrument owes its existence, he passes by without condemnation. Yet they are of a character peculiarly worthy the notice of a Chief Magistrate, for they affect the purity and value of the elective franchise. Their tendency is to dethrone the ballot-box, to make our elections a mockery, to substitute for the will of the people the decisions of party cabals and the designs of party leaders. If by false returns, fictitious votes, and the arbitrary arithmetic of officers of elections, the ballot-box be made to say one thing, whilst the people mean another, the sooner that ingenious little machine is abolished the better. The English viva voce plan, or mere virtual representation, without any voting at all, would be safer and far more honest. Yet by these fraudulent arts the politics of Kansas have been managed, from the Missouri election of the first Territorial Legislature, to the vote on the Lecompton Constitution. All this was in evidence before the President. The very men he successively appointed to carry out his policy in Kansas, told him of it, and proclaimed it to the world. Nevertheless, the Territorial Legislature and its laws, the Lecompton Constitution and the vote by which it was passed, are all upheld by the President, sanctioned, approved, and presented to Congress for ratification. Violence and fraud and ballot-box gambling are thus justified by the highest authority in the nation. It is an evil thing for any one to withhold praise or blame where either is due, because it is unjust, and because these are powerful influences to repress crime and encourage virtue. Still worse is it to give to crime that approval and support which belong of right only to virtue; and this should more especially be avoided by those whose high station adds weight and importance to their opinion, more sometimes than it deserves. Therefore a wise king, who well understood the duty and responsibility of his office, has written: "He that saith unto the wicked, Thou art righteous; him shall the people curse, nations shall abhor him."

Nevertheless, one argument used by the President is conclusive. He says that he is in favor of admitting Kansas under the Lecompton Constitution, because "This will carry out the great principle of non-intervention, recognized and sanctioned by the organic act, which declares in express language in favor of the 'non-intervention of Congress with slavery in the Territories,' leaving the people 'perfectly free to form and regulate their domestic institutions in their own way, subject only to the Constitution of the United States.'" This is true. If the Kansas and Nebraska Act be the law of the land—and such it is till repealed, or declared unconstitutional by the Supreme Court—Congress is bound to accept the Lecompton Constitution. That act places the Territories beyond the power of Congress, and wholly under the control of the local Legislature and the President. Kansas presents herself with a Constitution, which, the President declares, was made according to law, by the regularly constituted authorities of the Territory. The Convention was legally elected, he says; the Territorial Legislature was a genuine and valid Legislature. What right has Congress then, which has abdicated all authority over the Territories, to disregard, to discredit, these official declarations? What the President says, moreover, is true. The Legislature, the Convention, the Constitution, are all invested with legal form. It is true also, indeed, that this legal form is mere form, —sheep's clothing, beneath which there is a wolf. It is true also, that this Constitution is no more the act and will of the people of Kansas than of the people of England; that the Territorial Legislature represented not them, but Missouri; that the Convention was the mere tool of the South; that from first to last, every step in this shameful history was vitiated by fraud, tainted with corruption, often stained with blood. But what is that to Congress? The new law declares that the people of a Territory shall be "perfectly free to form and regulate their own institutions in their own way;" and the President, a constituent part of the government of the Territories, declares officially, that the Lecompton Constitution and Slavery are the institutions the people of Kansas have chosen to form, and in a "way" that is at once legal and their own. He asserts, moreover, that all those who opposed those "institutions," and that "way," are disaffected persons, rebels, and traitors, unworthy notice or regard. How then can Congress interfere? It may be said by some, that the Constitution of the United States has in it these words: "New States *may* be admitted by Congress into this Union," and that the word "may" would seem to imply some discretionary power over the subject in Congress,—some right to deliberate, to inquire into facts, to look through forms into substance, to disregard technicalities for the sake of merits, and finally to reject. But the answer to this is obvious. The Kansas and Nebraska Bill has altered this clause of the Constitution, and for "may," substituted "shall." For all the troubles in Kansas, therefore, the responsibility rests on the President, not on Congress; for he had legal power to prevent them, from the beginning, which Congress, by the new law, had not. He could have annulled the first Legislature, he could have vetoed its laws, he could have exerted his official influence in accordance with the wishes of the people, and, finally, he could have refused to present the Lecompton Constitution to Congress, in accordance with the promise made by himself and by the Governor appointed by him.

Such is the result of the first experiment in Territorial self-government and the practical effect of the conflicting principles of the new constitutional law, manufactured by the South. To be consistent with its promises and professions, this law should enable the people of a Territory to select their own Governor, Judges and Marshals, and thus have complete control over their political institutions, for in no other way can they be at liberty to form and regulate their domestic institutions. Had this been done, the Territories would be sovereign indeed, but their position would be so anomalous and absurd as to defy any ingenuity to define and understand it. Not States, with a complete apparatus of government for the management of their domestic concerns, and at the same time a proportionate power over the General Government, to which they are also subjected, they would be Independent Sovereignties, whose people formed part of another sovereignty, to which they owed no obedience, yet from which they would be entitled to claim protection. Independent Sovereignties, whose very soil was the property of another government, from which their people must buy and derive title to their land, which might therefore withhold it, and must "make all needful rules and regulations" respecting it. Being neither States nor subject to the Federal Government as Territories, they would, of course, have power to coin money, to lay imposts, to make treaties and war, to maintain an army and navy, and to establish any form of government they pleased, aristocracy, monarchy, or theocracy; or any domestic institutions they pleased, matrimony, slavery, polygamy, or socialism; or any religion they pleased, Christianity, Mahometism, Mormonism, or the worship of Juggernaut. They might also stay out of the Union, and maintain their independent position so long as they pleased, however populous and powerful they became. Of all this, Utah is an example. Its people are truly sovereign, according to the meaning of the Kansas and Nebraska Bill. They do really "form and regulate their own institutions in their own way." They have their own Governor and Legislature, and have expelled the Judges sent to them by the President, and thus they have been able to choose polygamy and theocracy, as their domestic institutions. In flagrant violation of the true principles of that bill, the President has sent bayonets to reduce them to obedience, just as he sent bayonets to reduce the people of Kansas to obedience. He has a right to do this as the bill now stands, because he is an important part of the Government of the Territories; but he is an institution they did not choose, and over which they have no control, and his power is inconsistent with the spirit of the law, which, if meant to be carried out fairly, should be altered to conform to that spirit.

It would be better, however, to repeal it altogether. The old law worked well. Under it there was no complaint. Under it many flourishing States have been admitted into the Union without trouble or disturbance, in or out of Congress. It is undoubtedly true that Congress might, if disposed to abuse its power, vexatiously interfere in the affairs of a Territory, or unreasonably refuse to admit it as a State. So might Congress, by a similar abuse, misgovern and oppress the District of Columbia. Yet the people of the District, as well as of the Territories, have, on the whole, been satisfied. They have, on the whole, been governed justly. Their interests, their wishes, their feelings have been considered and respected. But what is the security, it may be asked, that this shall continue? The best security the case admits of, and the only one: the principles of liberty on which our government is founded, and the public opinion of the country. Change these, and the security vanishes for the District, the Territories, and the States. So long as the people are animated by a republican spirit, Congress will represent that spirit, and govern the Territories in a republican manner; that is to say, according to the wishes of their people. The people of the Territories, though not represented in Congress directly, are virtually represented, because the great constituency of the country has rights, interests, and hopes similar to their own, and should these be injured by Congress, would make common cause with them, and through the press and the ballot-box, exercise its power to redress the wrong, as it is doing now. Power is from its very nature liable to abuse. If surrounded by too many restraints to prevent misgovernment, it ceases to be power. The chances of abuse are not diminished but increased, by placing the control of the Territories in the hands of the President, to whom the Kansas and Nebraska Bill gives it, instead of leaving it in Congress, to whom it was intrusted by the Constitution.

The just and wise management of the Territories in accordance with their wishes and their true interests, is the object to be attained, all will agree. It can only be attained by some sort of government. That which the Constitution provided and heretofore in use, gave to the Territories executive and judicial officers, appointed by the President, a local legislature, whose acts were subject to the revision of Congress, and a delegate in Congress, to make known the wishes of the people. This government was symmetrical and consistent. The Territories were subjected to a government which represented the sentiment and opinion of the Union, whilst ample means were provided for the expression of their own sentiment and opinion. Even to this mild control they were subjected only for a short time. This government was successful. The Territories have not complained, neither has the District of Columbia, placed under a more rigid rule, and placed under it forever. The Kansas and Nebraska Bill has abolished this government. It professes to erect in its stead the absolute sovereignty of the Territories, it promises to their people self-government, yet it does not perform its promise. It withdraws them from the power of Congress, yet leaves them to the power of the President. It takes away from them republican and gives them monarchial government. This government has also been tried, but it has not succeeded. On the contrary, the President is now, and has been for more than a year, employed in compelling the people, and by military force, to submit to laws and to accept institutions against their earnest protest and remonstrance. To carry out the meaning and fulfil the promise of the new law, the power of the President should also be withdrawn from the Territories. They would then be really sovereign, but they would also be independent nations; a position wholly inconsistent with the ownership of their soil by the Government of the Union, and with the fact that they form part of this Nation. This plan has also been tried, practically though not theoretically, and the result has been, Brigham Young and the rebellion in Utah, and another occasion for the President to employ soldiers to enforce his authority. Which then of these three plans ought to be preferred, the one sanctioned by time, success, and the Constitution, or either of the two which have failed?

Had the Constitution remained unaltered there would have been no trouble in Kansas. It would not have been thrown open as an arena for sectional strife. Its Legislature would not have been elected by Missouri votes, or, if it had, Congress would have declared the election void. The infamous Kansas laws would never have been enacted, or, if they were, Congress would have repealed them. The people would have voted for the Convention that made the Constitution, and Kansas would have been admitted as a Free State, without opposition or excitement, because its soil and climate fit it for free labor, and because its people prefer free labor. Why then was the Constitution altered? For the sake of the Territories? They did not ask for the change. It was not at the instance of the people of Kansas that the Kansas and Nebraska Bill was passed. All the Territories were tranquil and content under the old law. The change was made by the South, with the aid of the Northern Democracy, for Southern objects. Its purpose was to make Kansas a Slave State,—an impossibility; as a means of realizing the Southern dream of equality with the North,—another impossibility. It was obvious, from the first, that Kansas never could become a Slave State, and it is still more obvious that the power of the South in this Union can never equal that of the North. Political power depends on wealth, numbers, and the diffusion of comfort and education among the masses. In all these conditions, the superiority of the North, already so vast, is growing rapidly greater every day. Hopelessly and so long as this Union lasts, the South is doomed to be a minority, but not on that account to weakness or degradation. Destroy sectional animosity, banish the mischievous idea that there is a North or a South, and the inferiority disappears. So long as the South is able to secure the friendship and support of a great party in the North, and this it has always done, it may defend its rights and often control the Government, as it now does. It controls, at this moment, the Executive, the Legislature, the Judiciary,—the sword and the purse of the Nation,—and this, too, in the midst of sectional excitement and division. Weak and a minority though it be, it is defended by the Constitution, by the Northern Democracy, and not by it alone, but by the national sentiment of the great mass of the Northern people. Through these it is safe, it is triumphant, it reigns. Without these it is feeble, defenceless, dependent. With these, though it may not always rule, it must always be secure; without them it must submit to be governed and perhaps oppressed. Disunion would be no remedy. Disunion is not separation. The South cannot put an ocean between its weakness and the powerful North, which must ever remain at its side, either in the Union or out of the Union, either a friend or an enemy; and, if an enemy, one that would find an ally on every farm, on every plantation, at every fireside in the South. The Union, the Constitution, and the friendship of the North; these are the pillars on which rest the peace, the safety, the independence of the South. Destroy them and the South may read its fate in the history of the

Italian Republics, which is a history of Southern weakness, opposed to Northern strength.

The extraordinary thing is, that for some years past, the South has been and now is sedulously employed in undermining this triple foundation of its power and safety. Its extravagant pretensions, its excesses, its crimes, are rapidly cooling the friendship of the North, converting it, indeed, into positive enmity. Its leading politicians are ever plotting and threatening disunion. The time may come when disunion will be proffered to them from the North, not as a vague and passionate threat, but as a positive and well-considered plan, backed by a force of public opinion which nothing can resist. They are also repealing the Constitution, introducing new doctrines into our national law—doctrines contrived to serve a special and immediate purpose, but which, once established, may plague their inventors. Ideas, principles, are sharp tools to play with, and he who uses them has need of a mind that can see far into the future and calculate remote consequences. This sort of mind was possessed by those who framed our Constitution for the union and safety, the happiness and prosperity, the greatness and glory, of both North and South. The principles they established have proved their long-sighted wisdom, both in the success which has attended the observance of those principles and the disasters which have followed a departure from them. The Southern politicians who have since dared to meddle with the work of these sages, have not improved it; and the new doctrines they have established as instruments to carry out their narrow views and sectional policy, will be turned against them with fatal effect. This very Kansas and Nebraska Bill is a case in point, to show how an unskilful engineer may be hoisted by his own petard. Its immediate object was to make Kansas a slave State, and thus gain two Senators for the South. It was expected that a majority of the people of Kansas would be in favor of slavery; it was feared that a majority of Congress might be opposed to slavery. If, therefore, Kansas could be freed from the control of Congress, all would be safe. But the event turned out exactly the reverse of this, and for such a contingency the artificers of the bill forgot to provide. As a consequence, they found that their machine would not work. But though defeated, they are not overcome. Two Democratic Senators can be secured by forcing upon Kansas the Lecompton Constitution. They have the President, his message, and his patronage, and their hitherto faithful and well-drilled phalanx of Northern Democrats in Congress. But here another unexpected misfortune has occurred, the consequence of another blunder. They left entirely out of their calculations the fact that men, even Northern Democrats, have a conscience; a mistake never made by those who framed the old law. Northern Democrats have long been growing lukewarm to the cause of the South, disgusted by late outrages, and this disgust has at length shown itself in open revolt. The very author of the Kansas and Nebraska Bill itself, so lately a trusted and chosen leader among Southern politicians, he who had

"Spoke like thunder on their side,
Been sworn their champion, bidding them depend
Upon his stars, his fortune, and his strength,"

has suddenly deserted them and joined their enemies. His example has been followed by other chiefs high in influence and renown, whilst the Democratic party throughout the North is leaving them by thousands; and it is manifest that this great ally, with whom they have so often marched to victory, can no longer be depended on. Ere long the South is likely to be left with no other defence but the Union it has weakened and the Constitution it has mutilated and defaced.

But the Kansas and Nebraska Bill was not intended merely to put slavery into Kansas. It is a weapon fashioned for other and richer fields of conquest. Texas is to be divided, so as to make more Southern States and Senators; Nicaragua is to be annexed; and already, in the vivid and creative imagination of the South, Cuba looms up above the horizon, rich in negroes, in the countless treasures of an exuberant soil, and in votes. In all these, slavery is already planted and growing with tropical luxuriance, not as a mere abstract right, existing only in contemplation of Dred Scott case law, but as an actual fact. Slaves are there and masters, and these masters, if allowed "to form and regulate their own domestic institutions in their own way," will choose slavery and slaves, beyond a doubt. But "whoso diggeth a pit shall fall therein, and he that setteth a trap shall be taken therein." Even here, it may and most probably will happen, that the Kansas and Nebraska Bill will disappoint its inventors. When the day comes for the division of Texas, for the annexation of Nicaragua and Cuba, the chances are, that the President of the United States will be a Northern man, not with Southern, but

Northern principles. By the new law, the President is a part, and a most influential part, of the government of a Territory, and what has occurred in Kansas, may again occur; the people on one side, the President, his patronage, and his army on the other, and we may then see the instructive drama of the present moment repeated. A minority of the people, supported by the President, presenting to Congress a Constitution prohibiting slavery; that Constitution being the work of a packed Convention, and a Legislature elected by fictitious votes, and bolstered up by Executive corruption. A minority insisting on legal forms, and demanding instant admission as a free State, though nine-tenths of the people who are not slaves are masters of slaves, and earnestly insist on their right to choose their own institutions, earnestly appeal to a fettered and powerless Congress for justice and protection. What would the South say to that? And what would they say to a President who should urge upon Congress to accept such a Constitution, who should denounce this protesting majority as rebels and traitors, and ask for troops, to enable him to force upon them a free Constitution against their will.

The makers of the Kansas and Nebraska law were clumsy workmen. They forgot to provide for the case of an Anti-slavery President. They will, perhaps, learn wisdom by experience.

> "To wilful men,
> The injuries that they themselves procure,
> Must be their school-masters."

Those who framed the Constitution, and laid the foundation of this Union, understood their business better. That Constitution was intended to protect the South, and has protected it. Southern politicians cannot improve it. For their own sakes, they had better let it alone.

CECIL.

www.ingramcontent.com/pod-product-compliance
Lightning Source LLC
LaVergne TN
LVHW021420110826
845150LV00007B/2008

* 9 7 8 1 4 2 5 5 0 9 0 3 3 *